GINGER

GINGER

INTRODUCTION BY PEPITA ARIS

southwater

This edition is published by Southwater

Southwater is an imprint of
Anness Publishing Limited
Hermes House
88–89 Blackfriars Road
London SE1 8HA
tel. 020 7401 2077
fax 020 7633 9499

Distributed in the UK by
The Manning Partnership
251–253 London Road East
Batheaston
Bath BA1 7RL
tel. 01225 852 727
fax 01225 852 852

Distributed in the USA by
Anness Publishing Inc.
27 West 20th Street
Suite 504
New York
NY 10011
tel. 212 807 6739
fax 212 807 6813

Distributed in Australia by
Sandstone Publishing
Unit 1
360 Norton Street
Leichhardt
New South Wales 2040
tel. 02 9560 7888
fax 02 9560 7488

All rights reserved. No part of this publication may be reproduced, stored in a retrieval system, or transmitted in any way or by any means, electronic, mechanical, photocopying, recording or otherwise, without the prior written permission of the copyright holder.

© 1996, 2000 Anness Publishing Limited

1 3 5 7 9 10 8 6 4 2

Publisher Joanna Lorenz
Senior Cookery Editor Linda Fraser
Cookery Editor Anne Hildyard
Designer Lilian Lindblom
Illustrations Anna Koska
Photographers Karl Adamson, Edward Allwright, Steve Baxter,
James Duncan, Michelle Garrett, Don Last and Michael Michaels
Recipes Alex Barker, Roz Denny, Nicola Diggins, Rafi Fernandez, Christine France,
Sarah Gates, Shirley Gill, Deh-Ta Hsiung, Sue Maggs, Liz Trigg and Steven Wheeler
Food for photography Carole Handslip, Wendy Lee and Jane Stevenson
Stylists Madeleine Brehaut, Hilary Guy, Maria Kelly, Blake Minton,
Kirsty Rawlings and Fiona Tillett

For all recipes, quantities are given in both metric and imperial measures and, where appropriate, measures are also given in standard cups and spoons. Follow one set, but not a mixture, because they are not interchangeable.

Previously published as *Cooking with Ginger*

Contents

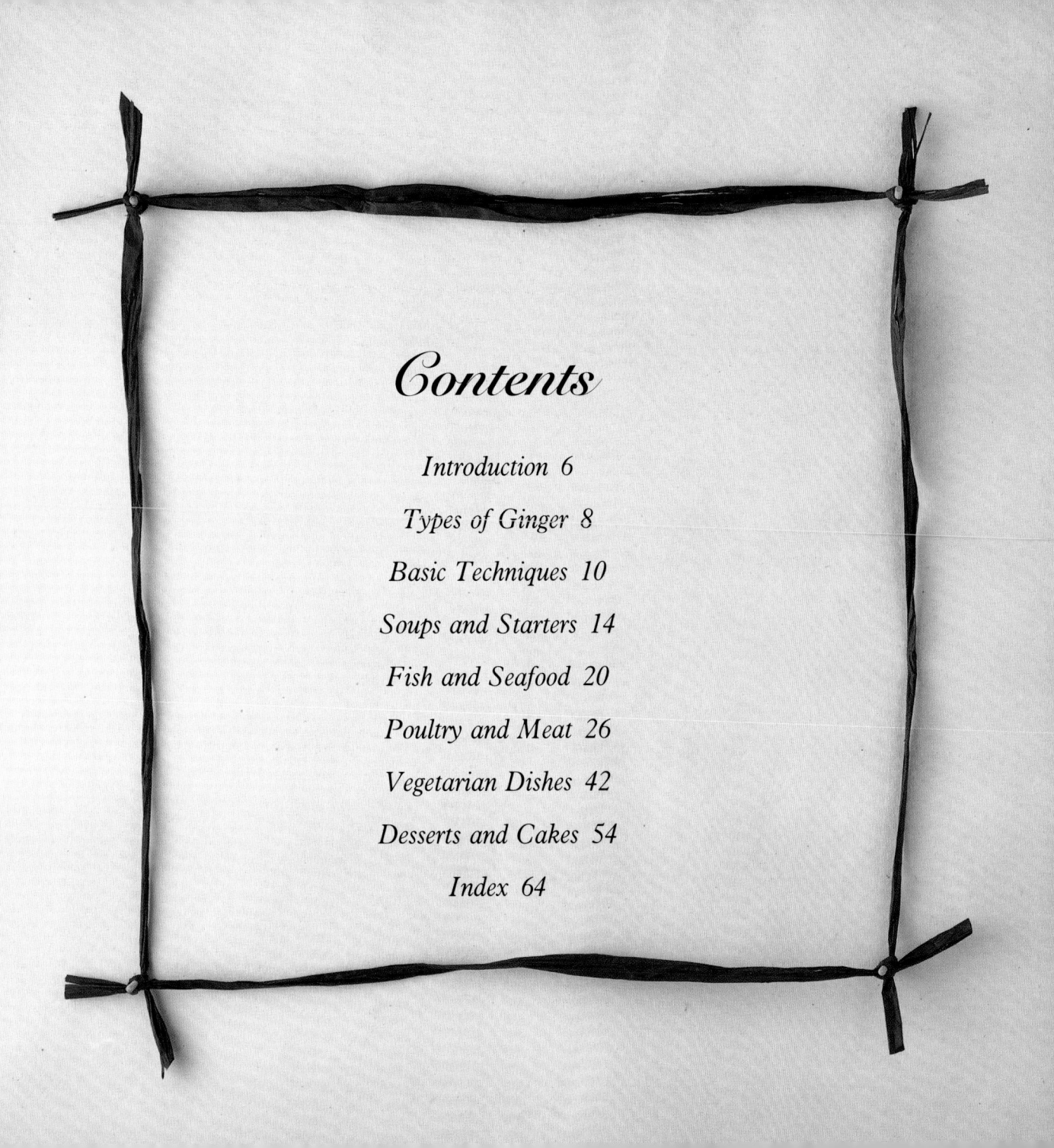

Introduction 6

Types of Ginger 8

Basic Techniques 10

Soups and Starters 14

Fish and Seafood 20

Poultry and Meat 26

Vegetarian Dishes 42

Desserts and Cakes 54

Index 64

Introduction

Who has not stopped to savour the delicious smell of ginger cooking? Whether it's the comforting and homely aroma of gingerbread baking on a winter's day or an intriguing burst of oriental promise, ginger has immediate appeal at all meals, sweet and savoury, all the year round.

Ginger has been a kitchen staple for more than a millennium – its use in Chinese cooking dates back to 200BC. Powdered ginger journeyed to Northern Europe early; it is the one Asiatic spice which predates introduction by the Crusaders. Its associations were, historically, wintry: bringing cheer at the coldest, dreariest time of year. Gingerbread is one of the oldest cake-breads in the world and is now found in every northern country, usually associated with Christmas and other winter festivals. Stem ginger, preserved in syrup in handsome blue and white jars that are now prized in their own right, came to Europe early in the eighteenth century from China.

Of course, ginger is used in most of Asia, and its flavour is central to the characteristic spice blends of a wide variety of oriental cuisines. Spring onions, ginger and garlic are the classic note of Chinese recipes; in India, the combination of ginger with onions and garlic is evident equally in North Indian sauces and in the vegetarian dishes that are the delight of southern states such as Gujarat. Powdered ginger is included in spice mixes and is popular in the rich dishes of Mogul cuisine – as it is, incidentally, in Moroccan cooking, one of the most refined of North Africa. And as Japanese and South-East Asian cooking become more popular all over the world, the popularity of ginger has increased.

Ginger is sold as a fresh root, dried whole, ground to powder, preserved in syrup and crystallized. Each form has a subtly different flavour, but common to all is a sweet and pungent spiciness.

The recipes in the book use all the forms to their best advantage and draw inspiration from all over the world. They begin with simple yet exotic soups and starters. In the next chapter, ginger adds sparkle to fish and shellfish recipes. Then meat and poultry dishes draw on ginger's incredibly varied international heritage. Vegetarian ideas carry on the theme, enlivening grains and vegetables with the refreshing taste of ginger. Lastly comes a luscious array of desserts and cakes, rounding off a mouth-watering exploration of the versatility and deliciousness of this unique spice.

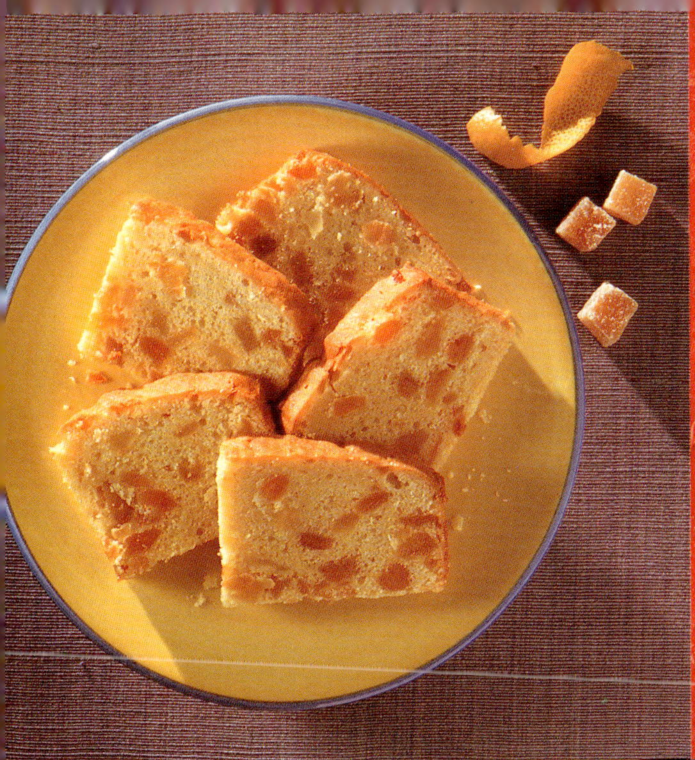
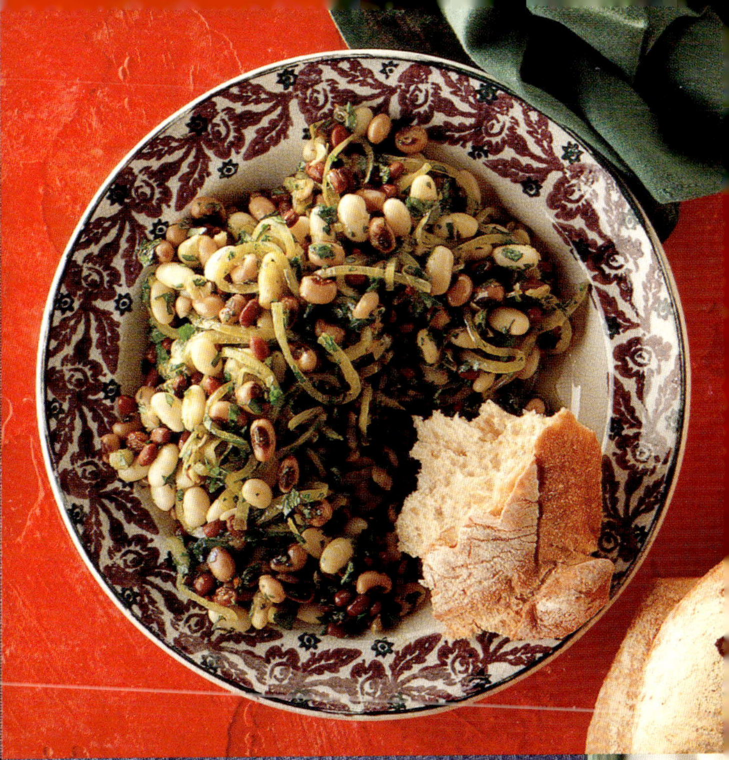
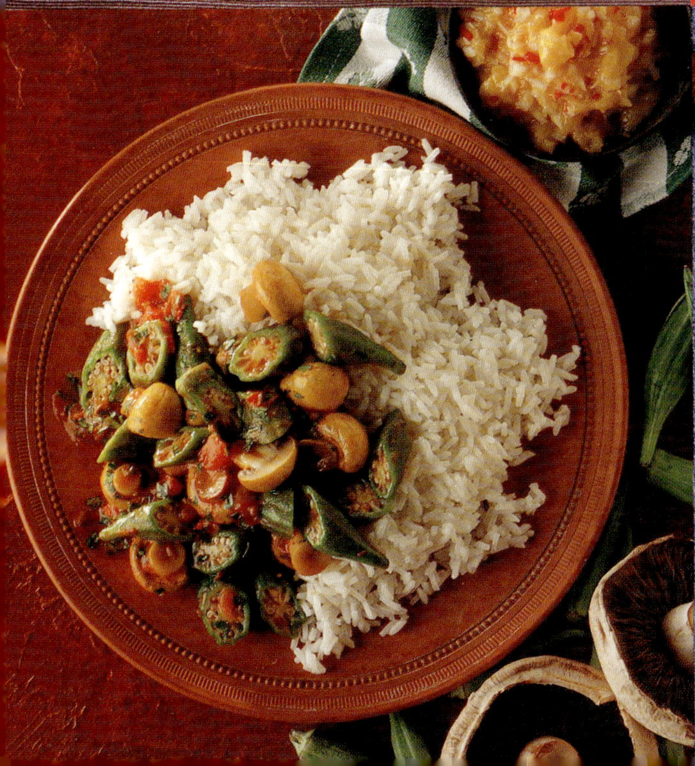
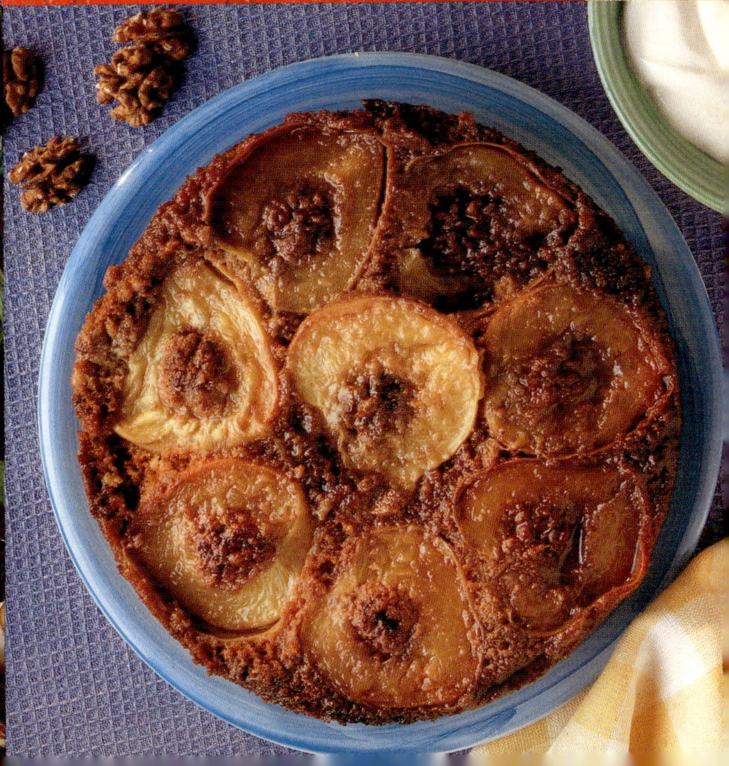

Types of Ginger

Fresh root ginger
A fresh knobbly root with a smooth, plump appearance and a pale tan-coloured skin. Any wrinkling indicates that the ginger is past its best. Once the skin has been peeled away, the ginger is a pale yellowy colour and should be firm to the touch, with a fresh, spicy fragrance. The most delicate flesh of the ginger is just below the skin; under this layer it becomes tougher with a slightly woody texture.

Dried root ginger
This is very different from the fresh form, and is no substitute for fresh root ginger. The whole root can be used in mixtures of pickling spices and requires bruising to release the flavour.

Crystallized ginger
Ginger is preserved in sugar syrup and then thickly coated in crystallized sugar and used as a flavouring in baking, or added to desserts such as ice cream.

Ground ginger
The ground form of dried ginger root, it has a hot, spicy flavour and is an essential spice in cakes, gingerbread and ginger biscuits. It is also used in savoury dishes such as curries and soups, often in combination with other spices.

Stem ginger
Tender, young shoots of ginger are cooked and preserved in sugar syrup. Both the ginger and the syrup can be used in cakes, sauces and ice cream. The syrup can be added to marinades for savoury dishes to give a sweet, gingery flavour.

Pickled ginger
Thin slices of ginger are preserved in sweetened vinegar and are used as a garnish for raw fish and served with sushi and other oriental foods. It has a very peppery, pungent flavour, and if added to a dish for its flavour, is removed before serving.

Sliced root ginger

Dried root ginger

Fresh root ginger

Pickled ginger

Ginger pulp

Crystallized ginger

Stem ginger

Fresh root ginger

Ground ginger

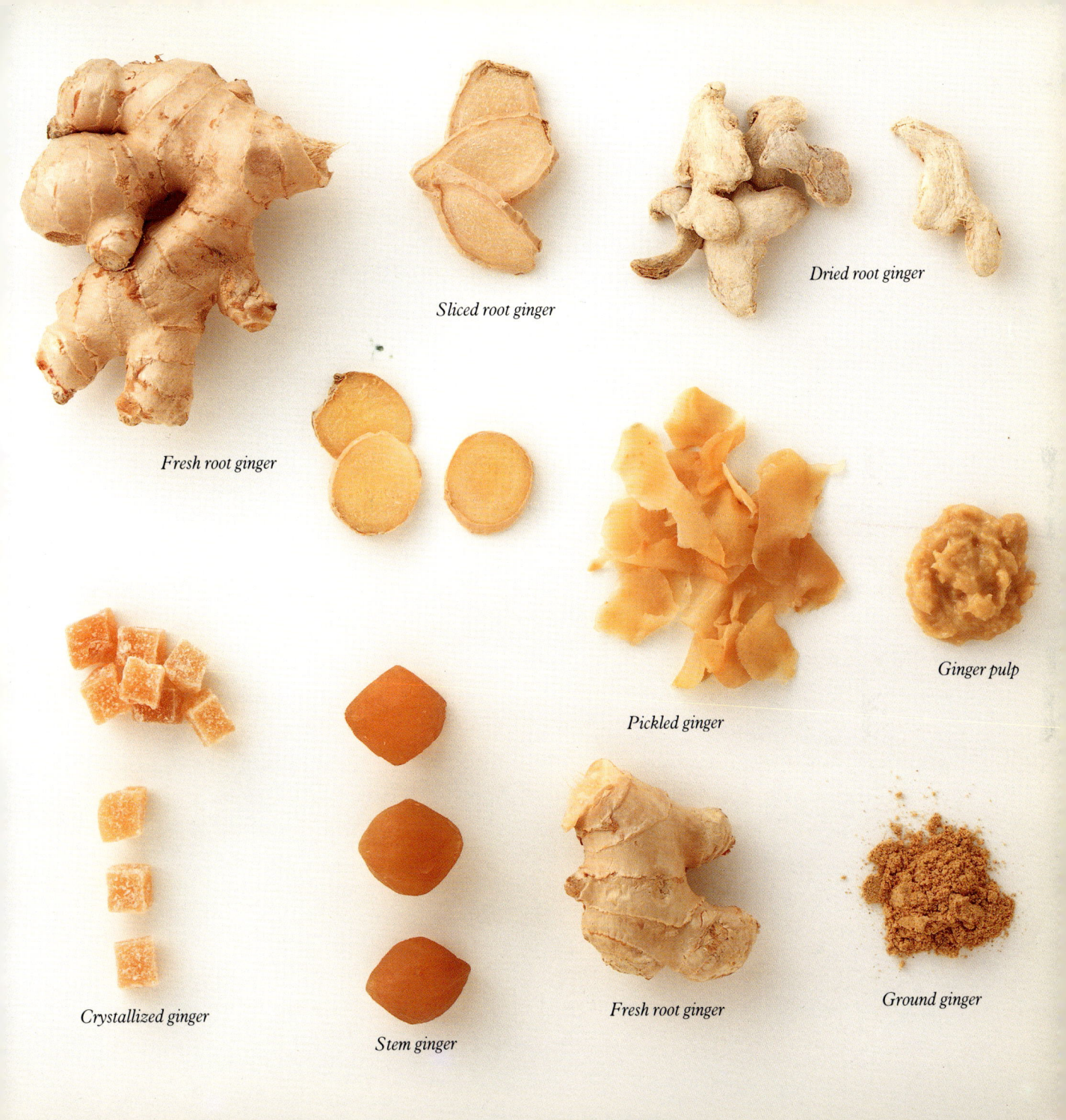

Basic Techniques

Preparing Root Ginger

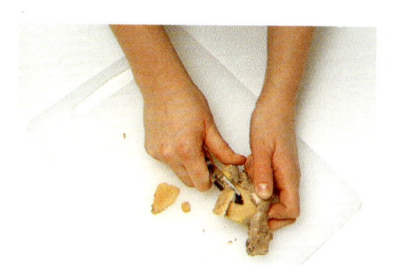

Break up the ginger into easily peelable pieces, avoiding very knobbly areas. Using a small sharp knife or vegetable peeler, peel off the skin very thinly and discard. The skin should be smooth and blemish free.

When adding to a recipe during cooking, slice the ginger. After peeling the ginger, cut into thin slices with a sharp knife.

If the root ginger is to be used as a flavouring at the beginning of a recipe, chop finely. When the ginger is to be stir-fried with other ingredients or used as a garnish for finished dishes, cut first into slices, then into fine julienne strips.

Root Ginger Tips

- *Buying fresh root ginger*: choose plump ginger with firm flesh and thin, smooth skin.

- *Storage*: unpeeled root ginger will keep for up to four weeks in the salad drawer of the fridge if wrapped tightly in clear film. Once it begins to wrinkle and take on a dry appearance, discard.

- *Grating*: peel the ginger, then grate finely. Add to sauces, soups, stews and marinades. Chop, grate or slice as required. 2.5cm/1in fresh root ginger yields about 15ml/1 tbsp finely chopped root ginger.

- If the ginger sprouts, chop the sprouts and use as a herb, added to salads.

BASIC TECHNIQUES

MAKING GINGER PULP

Ginger is often used in savoury recipes and it can be time-consuming to peel and process it everytime. It's much easier to make the pulp in large quantities and use as needed. To store the pulp, either transfer to an airtight container or jar and refrigerate for 4 to 6 weeks, or freeze in ice-cube trays kept specially for the purpose. Add 5ml/1 tsp of the pulp to each cube space, freeze, then remove from the tray and store in the freezer in a polythene bag. Remove the pulp when needed, and add, while still frozen, to curries or stews.

Peel about 225g/8oz fresh root ginger and place in a food processor or blender. Process until pulped, adding a little water to get the right consistency, if necessary.

Cook's Tips

- Ground ginger is included in many spice mixtures, the most common being mixed spice. It is also often added to 5-spice powder, a Chinese seasoning and appears in pickling spice mixtures.

- Together with ground black pepper, dried or fresh sage and rosemary, ground ginger makes a tasty poultry seasoning.

- An aromatic tea can be made by adding dried ginger to boiling water.

- Fresh root ginger, together with garlic and onion, is mainly used in stir-fries, oriental, Indian and Arab dishes. It has recently become equally popular in Western countries where it is often added to marinades and used to ginger up fish and poultry dishes.

BASIC TECHNIQUES

COOKING WITH GINGER

If the fresh root ginger is to be used in a stir-fry, heat the wok, then add the oil. When the oil is hot, add the chopped or grated ginger and any other ingredients and stir-fry for 30 seconds until the ginger is just golden brown.

Ginger juice, made from fresh root ginger, is good in marinades, sauces and salad dressings. To make ginger juice, crush finely chopped or grated fresh ginger in a garlic press and collect the juice in a bowl.

To make a simple curry paste, blend fresh root ginger with garlic, chilli and a little water.

QUICK DESSERTS

- Add 15ml/1 tbsp chopped stem ginger to fresh, cubed melon with a little of the syrup.

- Chop stem ginger and sprinkle over poached fruit such as peaches, pears or apples.

- Dice a piece of stem ginger very finely, add to soft icing, and use for icing cakes or biscuits.

- Add a little finely chopped stem ginger to whipped cream and serve with fruit, a baked crumble, or a steamed pudding.

- Chop some crystallized ginger finely and add to cream or cream cheese, and use as a cake filling.

- Stir some finely chopped stem or crystallized ginger into whipped cream. Use as a sandwich filling for plain meringues.

BASIC TECHNIQUES

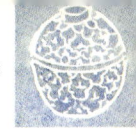

FLAVOURING WITH GINGER

• Ground ginger and crystallized ginger are used in traditional recipes for gingerbread and ginger biscuits.

• Preserved ginger in syrup can be used as a flavouring in baking and added to ice cream and other desserts. It is also delicious in cakes, mousses and sauces, and even savoury dishes. Stem ginger is specially selected for preservation, being made from the choicest, most tender shoots from the ginger root.

RHUBARB AND GINGER JAM   Makes about 1.75kg/4lb

Ginger and rhubarb are the perfect flavour combination in this spicy, tart jam.

Place 15ml/1 tbsp grated, fresh root ginger and 1.25kg/2¾lb trimmed rhubarb into a preserving pan. Add 1.12kg/2½lb granulated sugar, the rind and juice of half a lemon, and two peeled, cored and diced cooking apples. Cover the pan and cook over gentle heat until the sugar has melted and the fruits have yielded liquid. When the sugar has completely dissolved, uncover and boil until the temperature reaches the jam setting point on a sugar thermometer, 107°C/225°F. Or transfer a small spoonful of jam to a cold saucer, cool a little, then gently push the jam with a finger. If set, it will wrinkle.

Soups and Starters

Fresh ginger makes an aromatic addition to all sorts of first courses – it adds a spicy fragrance to even the simplest soup, and its distinctive flavour is perfect in oriental-style starters.

Leek, Parsnip and Ginger Soup

A flavoursome winter warmer, with the added spiciness of fresh ginger.

Serves 4–6

30ml/2 tbsp olive oil
225g/8oz leeks, sliced
30ml/2 tbsp finely chopped fresh root ginger
675g/1½lb parsnips, roughly chopped
300ml/½ pint/1¼ cups dry white wine
1.2 litres/2 pints/5 cups vegetable stock or water
salt and ground black pepper
soured cream, to garnish
paprika, to garnish

Heat the oil in a large pan and add the leeks and ginger. Cook gently for 2–3 minutes, until the leeks start to soften. Add the parsnips and cook for a further 7–8 minutes.

Pour in the wine and stock or water and bring to the boil. Reduce the heat and simmer for 20–30 minutes or until the parsnips are tender.

Purée in a food processor or blender until smooth. Season to taste. Reheat and garnish with a swirl of soured cream and a light dusting of paprika.

Cook's Tip
For an extra gingery flavour, garnish the soup with very finely shredded root ginger.

Thai Chicken and Prawn Soup

Fresh ginger adds a sharp, refreshing tang to this hot and spicy soup.

Serves 4–6

2 chicken breasts, 175g/6oz each, on the bone
½ chicken stock cube
400g/14oz can coconut milk
7.5cm/3in piece lemon grass
15ml/1 tbsp chopped fresh root ginger
2 garlic cloves, crushed
30ml/2 tbsp chopped coriander root, or stem
2–3 small red chillies, seeded and finely chopped
30ml/2 tbsp fish sauce
25ml/5 tsp sugar
2.5ml/½ tsp salt
2 lime leaves
225g/8oz fresh or cooked prawns, peeled and deveined
juice of 1 lime
4 coriander sprigs, chopped, to garnish
2 spring onions, green part only, sliced, to garnish
4 large red chillies, sliced, to garnish

Place the chicken in a large saucepan and just cover with cold water. Add the half stock cube, and bring to the boil, then reduce the heat and simmer for 45 minutes. Lift the chicken out of the cooking liquid and set the liquid aside. Discard the skin and bones from the chicken and slice the meat into strips. Return the shredded chicken to the cooking liquid, add the coconut milk and simmer gently.

Finely chop the lemon grass and place in a bowl with the ginger, garlic, coriander and chillies. Mix thoroughly, then add to the cooking liquid with the fish sauce, sugar, salt and lime leaves. Simmer for a further 20 minutes.

Just before serving, add the prawns and lime juice. Simmer very gently for 5 minutes. Garnish with the coriander, spring onions and chillies.

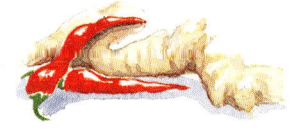

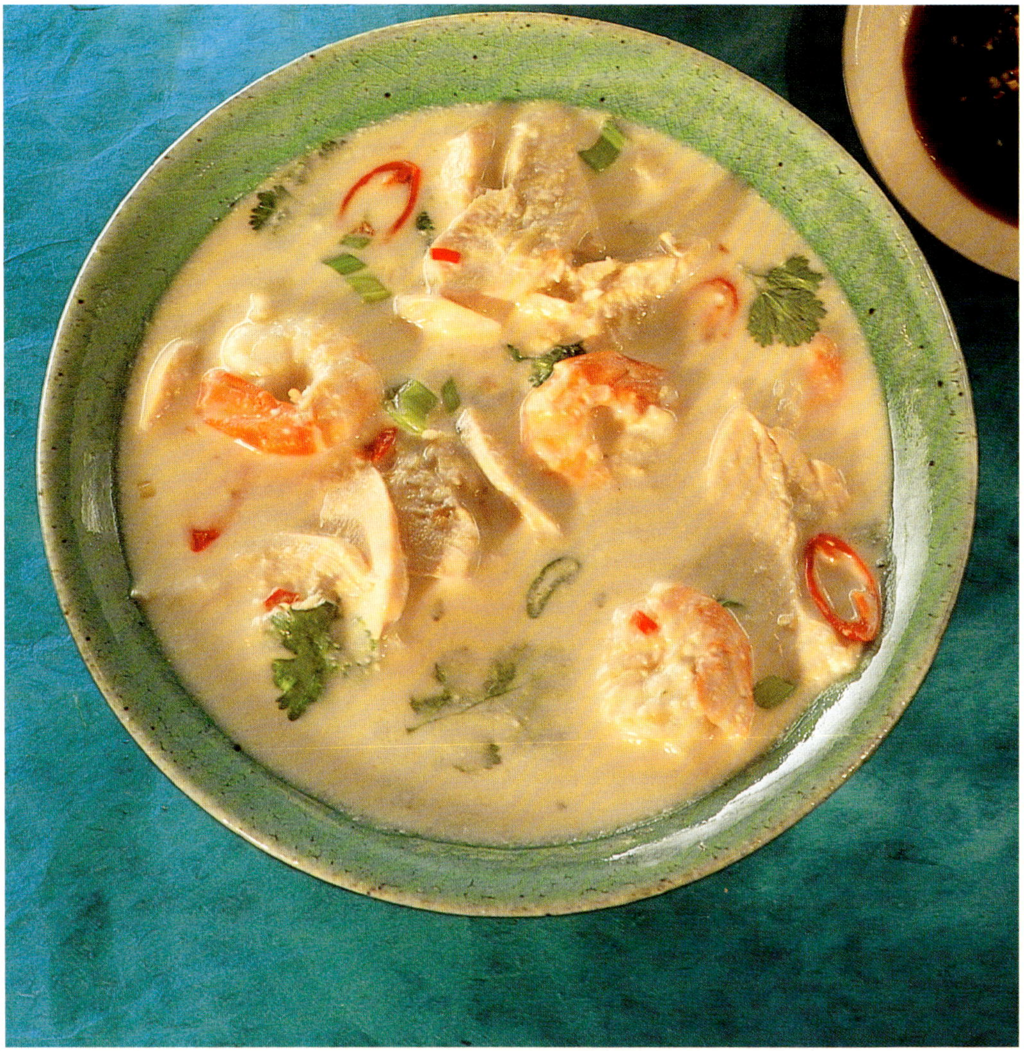

SOUPS AND STARTERS

GINGERY CHINESE CHICKEN WINGS

These are best eaten with fingers as a first course, so make sure you provide plenty of paper napkins.

Serves 4

12 chicken wings
3 garlic cloves, crushed
30ml/2 tbsp grated fresh root ginger
juice of 1 large lemon
45ml/3 tbsp soy sauce
45ml/3 tbsp clear honey
2.5ml/½ tsp chilli powder
150ml/¼ pint/⅔ cup chicken stock
salt and ground black pepper
lemon wedges, to garnish

Remove the tips from the chicken wings and use to make the stock. Cut the wings into two joints. Mix the garlic, ginger, lemon juice, soy sauce, honey and chilli powder together and coat the chicken wings in the mixture. Season to taste, cover with clear film and marinate overnight.

Preheat the oven to 220°C/425°F/Gas 7. Remove the chicken wings from the marinade and arrange in a single layer in a roasting tin. Bake for 20–25 minutes, basting at least twice with the marinade until it is used up.

Place the chicken wings on a serving plate. Add the stock to the marinade in the roasting tin, and bring to the boil.

Cook to a syrupy consistency and spoon a little of the sauce over the wings. Serve hot, garnished with lemon wedges.

COOK'S TIP

If you prefer, use chicken breasts or drumsticks instead of chicken wings. Bake until the juices run clear when the flesh is pierced with a skewer.

Spicy Peanut and Ginger Bites

Serve these spicy rice balls with a crisp green salad and a dipping sauce as a starter or snack.

Makes 16

1 garlic clove, crushed
15ml/1 tbsp finely chopped fresh root ginger
1.5ml/¼ tsp ground turmeric
5ml/1 tsp sugar
2.5ml/½ tsp salt
5ml/1 tsp chilli sauce
10ml/2 tsp fish or soy sauce
30ml/2 tbsp chopped fresh coriander
juice of ½ lime
115g/4oz/½ cup long grain rice, cooked
50g/2oz unsalted peanuts, chopped
150ml/¼ pint/⅔ cup vegetable oil, for deep-frying

Pound together the garlic, ginger and turmeric using a pestle and mortar. Add the sugar, salt, chilli and fish or soy sauce, coriander and lime juice.

Add three quarters of the cooked rice and pound until smooth and sticky. Stir in the rest of the rice. Wet your hands and shape into thumb-size balls.

Roll the balls in chopped peanuts so they are coated evenly. Set aside until ready to cook and serve.

Heat the vegetable oil in a deep frying pan. Prepare a tray lined with kitchen paper to drain the rice balls. Deep-fry a few at a time until crisp and golden, remove with a slotted spoon then drain on kitchen paper.

Fish and Seafood

Combined with other fragrant ingredients, such as lemon grass, lime and coriander, ginger brightens up marinades and adds a savoury spiciness to sauces for fish and shellfish.

Fish with Mango and Ginger Dressing

The tasty dressing for this salad combines the flavour of rich mango with ginger, hot chilli and lime.

Serves 4

1 French loaf
4 red mullet or snapper, each weighing about 275g/10oz
15ml/1 tbsp vegetable oil
1 mango
15ml/1 tbsp grated fresh root ginger
1 fresh red chilli, seeded and finely chopped
30ml/2 tbsp lime juice
30ml/2 tbsp chopped fresh coriander
175g/6oz young spinach
175g/6oz cherry tomatoes, halved, to garnish

Preheat the oven to 180°C/350°F/Gas 4. Cut the French loaf into 20cm/8in lengths. Slice lengthways, then cut into thick fingers. Place the bread on a baking sheet and dry in the oven for 15 minutes. Preheat the grill. Slash the fish on both sides and moisten with oil. Grill for about 6 minutes, turning once. Slice one half of the mango and reserve. Place the remainder in a blender or food processor. Add the ginger, chilli, lime juice and coriander. Process until smooth. Adjust to a pouring consistency with 30–45ml/2–3 tbsp water. Wash and dry the spinach, then arrange on four plates. Place the fish over the leaves. Spoon on the mango dressing and serve with mango slices, tomato halves, and the French bread.

Cook's Tip

Other varieties of fish that are suitable for this salad include salmon, monkfish, tuna, sea bass and halibut.

Grilled Snapper with Mango Salsa

A ripe mango is used in this fruity salsa with the tropical flavours of coriander, ginger and chilli.

Serves 4
350g/12oz new potatoes
3 eggs
115g/4oz French beans, topped, tailed and halved
4 × 350g/12oz red snapper, scaled and gutted
30ml/2 tbsp olive oil
175g/6oz mixed lettuce leaves, such as frisée or Webb's
2 cherry tomatoes
salt and ground black pepper

For the salsa
45ml/3 tbsp chopped fresh coriander
1 medium-size ripe mango, peeled, stoned and diced
½ red chilli, seeded and chopped
15ml/1 tbsp grated fresh root ginger
juice of 2 limes
generous pinch of celery salt

Bring the potatoes to the boil and simmer for 15–20 minutes. Drain. Bring a second large saucepan of salted water to the boil. Put in the eggs and boil for 4 minutes, then add the beans and cook for a further 6 minutes. Remove the eggs from the pan, cool, peel and cut into quarters. Preheat a moderate grill. Slash the snappers on each side, moisten with oil and cook for 12 minutes, turning once. To make the salsa, place the coriander in a blender or food processor. Add the remaining ingredients and process until smooth.

Arrange the lettuce on four large plates. Arrange the snapper over the lettuce and season to taste. Halve the potatoes and tomatoes, and add with the beans and eggs to the salad. Serve with the salsa.

SCALLOPS WITH GINGER RELISH

Scallops flavoured with spicy star anise are perfectly matched with a sharp and refreshing ginger relish.

Serves 4

8 king or queen scallops
4 whole star anise
25g/1oz/2 tbsp unsalted butter
salt and freshly ground white pepper
fresh chervil sprigs and whole star anise, to garnish

For the relish
½ cucumber, peeled
salt, for sprinkling
30ml/2 tbsp fresh root ginger
10ml/2 tsp caster sugar
45ml/3 tbsp rice wine vinegar
10ml/2 tsp ginger juice, strained from a jar of stem ginger
sesame seeds, for sprinkling

To make the relish, halve the cucumber lengthways and scoop out the seeds with a teaspoon. Cut the cucumber into 2.5cm/1in pieces, place in a colander and sprinkle with salt. Set aside for 30 minutes. To prepare the scallops, cut each into 2–3 slices. Coarsely grind the star anise in a pestle and mortar. Place the scallop slices with the corals in a bowl and marinate with the star anise and seasoning for about 1 hour. Rinse the cucumber under cold water and pat dry on kitchen paper. Cut the ginger into thin julienne strips and mix with the remaining relish ingredients. Cover and chill. Heat the butter in a wok. Add the scallop slices and stir-fry for 2–3 minutes. Garnish with sprigs of chervil and whole star anise, and serve with the cucumber relish, sprinkled with sesame seeds.

FISH AND SEAFOOD

Seafood Kebabs with Ginger and Lime

This fragrant marinade will guarantee a mouth-watering aroma from the barbecue, and it is equally delicious with chicken or pork.

Serves 4–6

500g/1¼lb prawns and cubed monkfish
selection of prepared vegetables, such as red, green or orange peppers, courgettes, button mushrooms, red onion, bay leaves, cherry tomatoes

For the marinade
3 limes
15ml/1 tbsp green cardamom pods
1 onion, finely chopped
15ml/1 tbsp grated fresh root ginger
1 large garlic clove, skinned and crushed
45ml/3 tbsp olive oil

First make the marinade. Finely grate the rind from one lime and squeeze the juice from all of them. Split the cardamom pods and remove the seeds. Crush the cardamom seeds in a pestle and mortar or with the back of a heavy-bladed knife.

Place the lime rind and juice, crushed cardamom, onion, root ginger, garlic and olive oil in a small bowl and mix together thoroughly. Pour the marinade over the prawns and monkfish, stir gently, then cover and leave in a cool place for 2–3 hours.

Thread four skewers alternately with the prawns, monkfish, vegetables and bay leaves. Cook slowly under a hot grill or over a barbecue, basting occasionally with the marinade, until the prawns, fish and vegetables are just cooked through and browned on the outside. Serve at once.

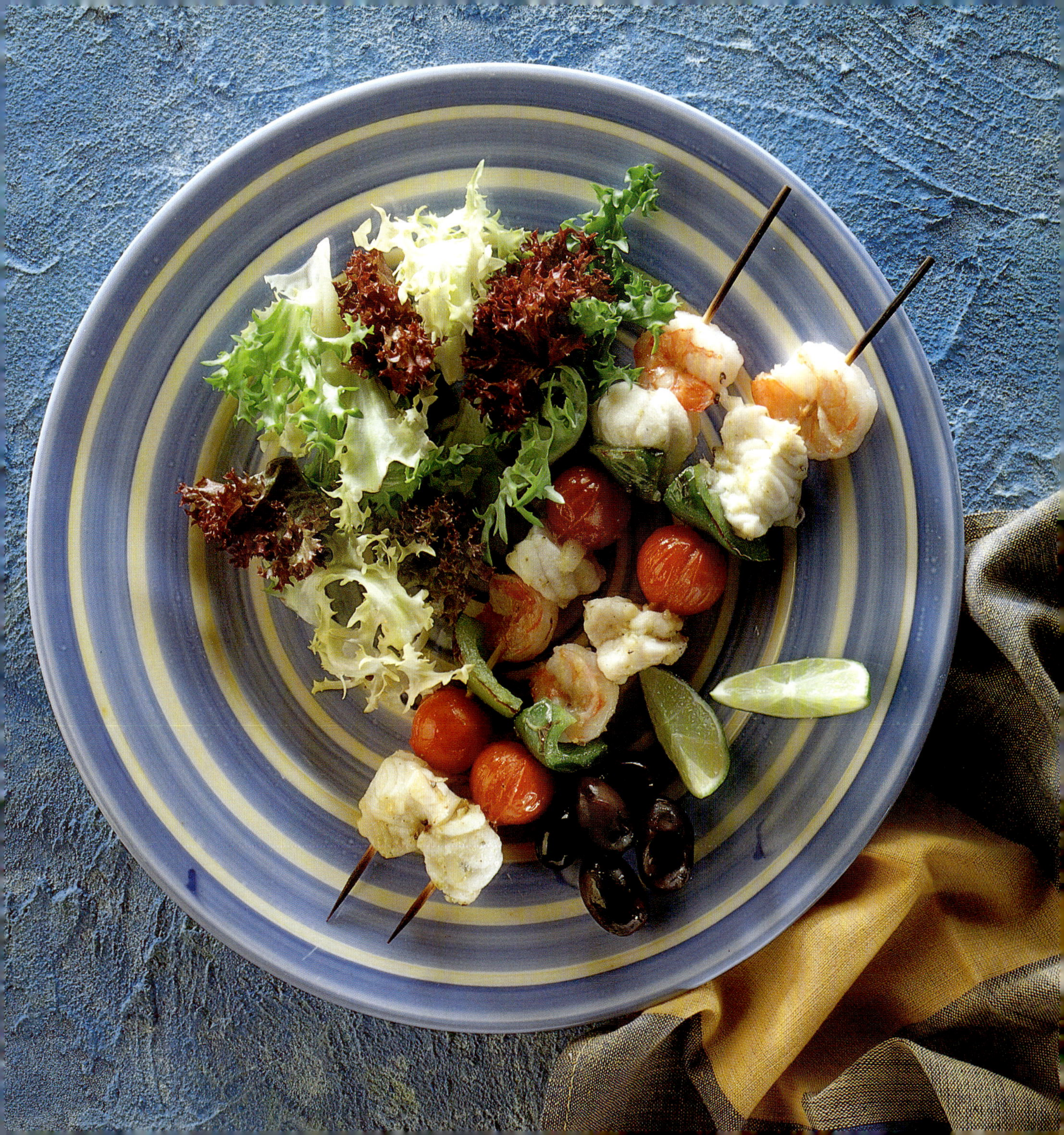

Poultry and Meat

Ginger is delicious with meat dishes. It is especially good with chicken, but is also excellent with beef, lamb and pork, adding a fresh flavour and warm spiciness to a variety of dishes.

Thai Chicken and Vegetable Stir-fry

Ginger and lemon grass add the authentic flavour of Thailand to this tasty stir-fry.

Serves 4

1 piece lemon grass (or the rind of ½ lemon)
30ml/2 tbsp sunflower oil
15ml/1 tbsp grated fresh root ginger
1 large garlic clove, chopped
275g/10oz lean chicken, thinly sliced
½ red pepper, seeded and sliced
½ green pepper, seeded and sliced
4 spring onions, chopped
2 medium carrots, cut into matchsticks
115g/4oz fine green beans
30ml/2 tbsp oyster sauce
pinch sugar
salt and ground black pepper
25g/1oz/¼ cup salted peanuts, lightly crushed, and coriander leaves, to garnish

Cook's tip
Make this quick supper dish a little hotter by adding more fresh root ginger, if you wish.

Thinly slice the lemon grass or lemon rind. Heat the oil in a frying pan over a high heat until hazy. Add the lemon grass or lemon rind, ginger and garlic, and stir-fry for 30 seconds until brown.

Add the chicken and stir-fry for 2 minutes. Then add the vegetables and stir-fry for 4–5 minutes, until the chicken is cooked and the vegetables are almost cooked.

Finally stir in the oyster sauce, sugar and seasoning to taste and stir-fry for another minute to mix and blend well. Serve at once, sprinkled with the peanuts and coriander leaves and accompanied with rice.

Chicken with Ginger Couscous

Couscous varies from country to country in North Africa. In this version, both the sauce and the grain are fragrantly spiced with cinnamon and ginger.

Serves 4

30ml/2 tbsp sunflower oil
4 chicken pieces
2 onions, finely chopped
2 garlic cloves, crushed
15ml/1 tbsp grated fresh root ginger
2.5ml/½ tsp ground cinnamon
1.5ml/¼ tsp ground turmeric
30ml/2 tbsp orange juice
10ml/2 tsp clear honey
salt and ground black pepper
fresh mint sprigs, to garnish

For the couscous
350g/12oz/2 cups couscous
5ml/1 tsp salt
10ml/2 tsp caster sugar
30ml/2 tbsp sunflower oil
2.5ml/½ tsp ground cinnamon
2.5ml/½ tsp ground ginger
30ml/2 tbsp sultanas
50g/2oz/½ cup blanched almonds
45ml/3 tbsp chopped pistachios

Heat the oil in a large pan and add the chicken pieces, skin side down. Fry for 3–4 minutes, until the skin is golden, then turn over.

Add the onions, garlic, ginger, spices and a pinch of salt. Add the orange juice and 300ml/½ pint/1¼ cups water. Cover and bring to the boil, then reduce the heat and simmer for about 30 minutes.

Meanwhile, place the couscous and salt in a bowl and cover with 350ml/12fl oz/1½ cups water. Stir once and leave to stand for 5 minutes. Add the caster sugar, 15ml/1 tbsp of the oil, the cinnamon, ginger and sultanas to the couscous and mix very well. Chop the almonds.

Heat the remaining 15ml/1 tbsp of the oil in a pan and lightly fry the almonds until golden. Stir into the couscous with the pistachios.

Line a steamer with greaseproof paper and spoon in the couscous. Sit the steamer over the chicken (or over a separate pan of boiling water) and steam for 10 minutes.

Remove the steamer and keep covered. Stir the honey into the chicken liquid and boil rapidly for 3–4 minutes. Spoon the couscous on to a warmed serving platter and top with the chicken and a little of the sauce spooned over. Garnish with mint sprigs and serve with the remaining sauce.

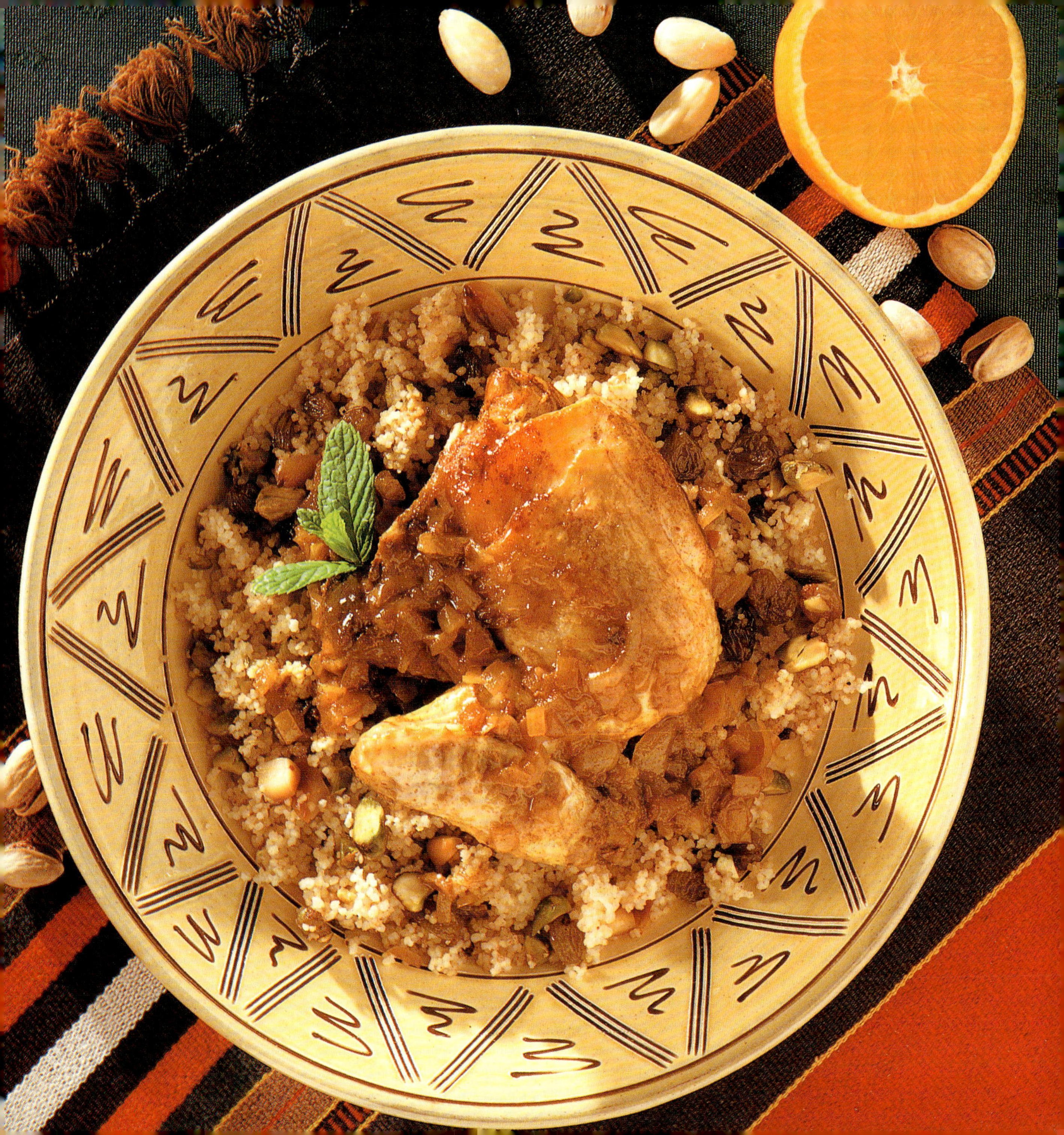

Stir-fried Ginger Chicken

This Southeast Asian-style stir-fry is colourful, quick to make, and full of flavour.

Serves 4

275g/10oz Chinese egg noodles
30ml/2 tbsp vegetable oil
3 spring onions, chopped
1 garlic clove, crushed
15ml/1 tbsp grated fresh root ginger
5ml/1 tsp hot paprika
5ml/1 tsp ground coriander
3 boneless chicken breasts, sliced
115g/4oz/1 cup sugar-snap peas, topped and tailed
115g/4oz baby sweetcorn, halved
225g/8oz/1 cup fresh beansprouts
15ml/1 tbsp cornflour
45ml/3 tbsp soy sauce
45ml/3 tbsp lemon juice
15ml/1 tbsp sugar
45ml/3 tbsp chopped fresh coriander or spring onion tops, to garnish

Bring a large saucepan of salted water to the boil. Add the noodles and cook according to the packet instructions. Drain, cover and keep warm.

Heat the oil in a wok or large frying pan. Add the spring onions and cook over a gentle heat for a minute or two. Add the garlic, root ginger, paprika, coriander and mix well, then stir in the chicken. Stir-fry for 3–4 minutes, then add the sugar-snap peas, baby sweetcorn and beansprouts and steam briefly. Add the noodles.

Combine the cornflour, soy sauce, lemon juice and sugar in a small bowl. Add to the wok or frying pan and simmer briefly to thicken, stirring all the time. Serve garnished with chopped coriander or spring onion tops.

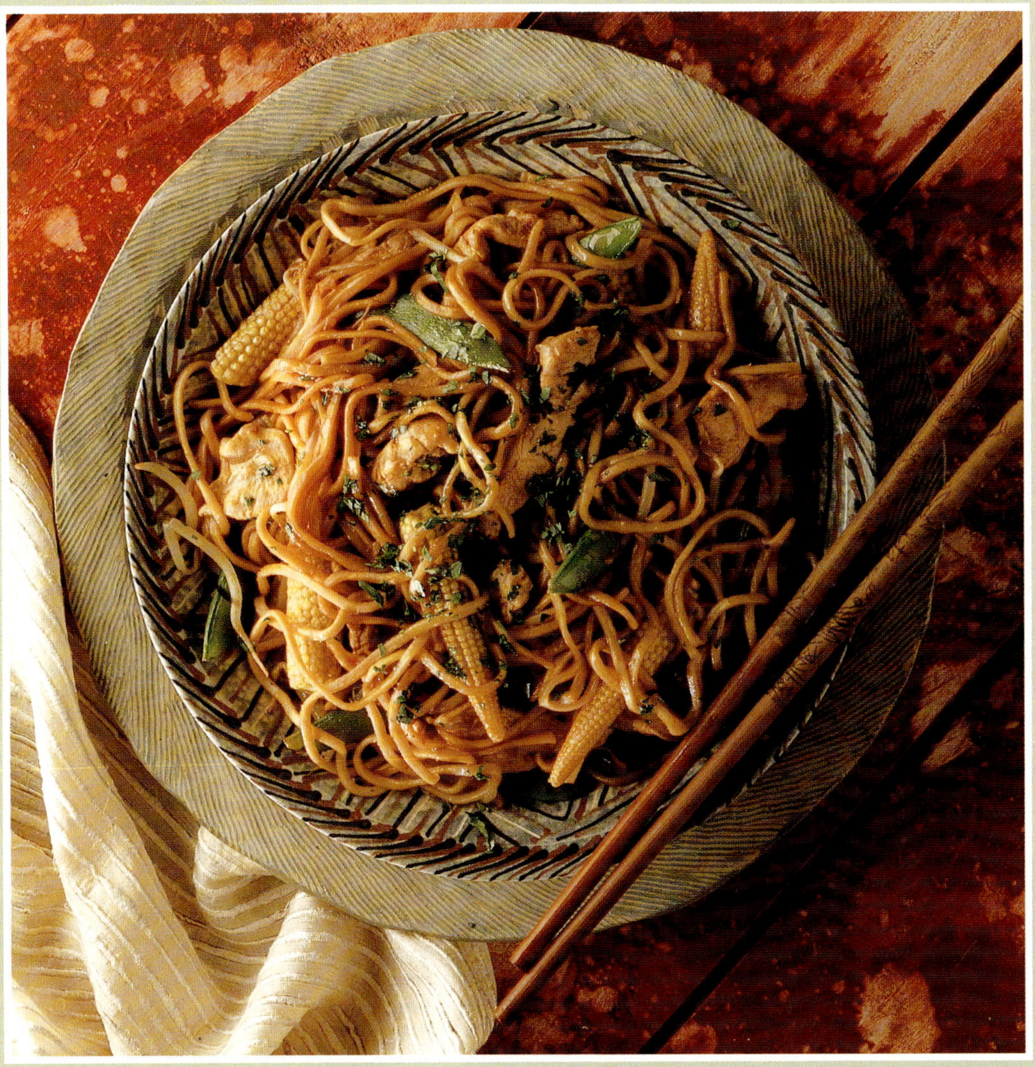

Chicken Biryani

A spiced Indian rice dish, flavoured with ginger and delicately scented with saffron, is layered with chicken and tomatoes, and is a favourite for special occasions.

Serves 4

275g/10oz/1½ cups basmati rice
2.5ml/½ tsp salt
5 whole green cardamom pods
2–3 whole cloves
1 cinnamon stick
45ml/3 tbsp vegetable oil
3 onions, sliced
675g/1½lb boneless, skinless chicken
1.5ml/¼ tsp ground cloves
2.5ml/½ tsp ground cardamom
1.5ml/¼ tsp hot chilli powder
5ml/1 tsp each ground cumin
  and coriander
2.5ml/½ tsp ground black pepper
3 garlic cloves, finely chopped
15ml/1 tbsp chopped fresh root ginger
juice of 1 lemon
4 tomatoes, sliced
30ml/2 tbsp chopped fresh coriander
150ml/¼ pint/⅔ cup natural yogurt
2.5ml/½ tsp saffron strands
45ml/3 tbsp toasted flaked almonds
  and fresh coriander sprigs, to garnish

Preheat the oven to 190°C/375°F/Gas 5. Bring a pan of water to the boil and add the rice, salt, cardamom pods, cloves and cinnamon stick. Boil for 2 minutes and then drain, leaving the whole spices in the rice.

Heat the oil in a pan and fry the onions for 8 minutes, until browned. Cube the chicken and add to the pan followed by all the ground spices, the garlic, ginger and lemon juice. Stir-fry for 5 minutes.

Transfer the chicken mixture to a casserole and lay the tomatoes on top. Sprinkle over the fresh coriander, spoon over the yogurt and top with the drained rice. Soak the saffron in 10ml/2 tsp hot milk, then drizzle over the rice and pour over 150ml/¼ pint/⅔ cup water.

Cover tightly and bake in the oven for 1 hour. Transfer to a warmed serving platter and remove the whole spices from the rice. Garnish with toasted almonds and fresh coriander. Serve with yogurt, if you like.

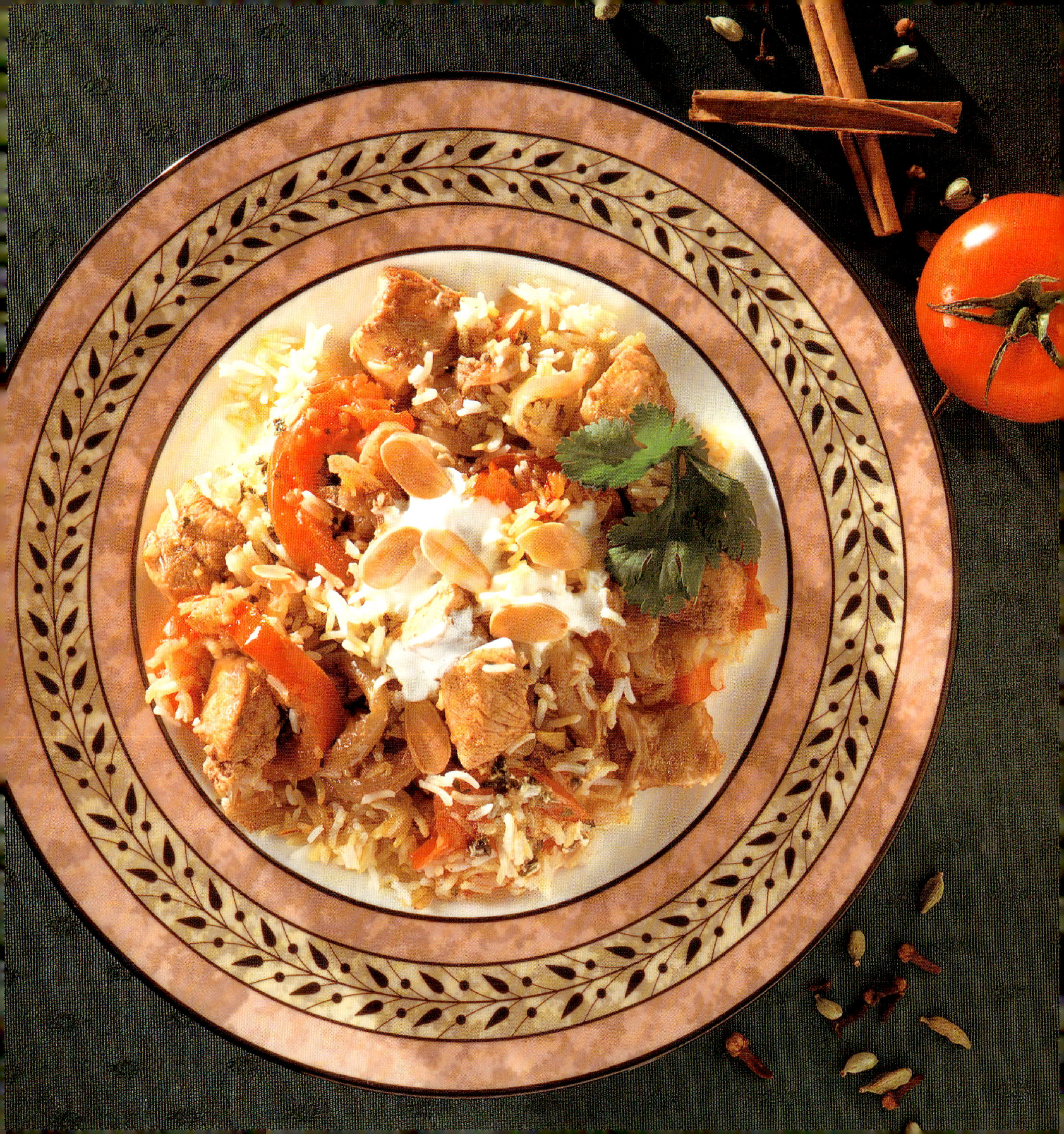

Chinese-style Beef with Ginger

Toasted sesame seeds and fresh ginger add an oriental flavour to this dish.

Serves 4
450g/1lb rump steak
30ml/2 tbsp sesame seeds
15ml/1 tbsp sesame oil
30ml/2 tbsp vegetable oil
115g/4oz small mushrooms, quartered
1 large green pepper, seeded and diced
4 spring onions, chopped diagonally

For the marinade
10ml/2 tsp cornflour
30ml/2 tbsp rice wine or sherry
15ml/1 tbsp lemon juice
15ml/1 tbsp soy sauce
few drops Tabasco sauce
15ml/1 tbsp grated fresh root ginger
1 garlic clove, crushed

Trim the steak and cut into thin strips roughly 1 × 5cm/½ × 2 in. Place the sesame seeds in a large frying pan or wok. Cook dry, over a moderate heat, shaking the pan until the seeds are golden. Set aside.

To make the marinade, blend the cornflour with the rice wine or sherry in a bowl, then stir in the lemon juice, soy sauce, Tabasco sauce, root ginger and garlic. Add the beef, stir thoroughly, then leave to marinate for 1–2 hours in the fridge.

Heat the oils in the frying pan or wok. Drain the beef, reserving the marinade, and brown a few pieces at a time. Remove the beef with a slotted spoon and keep warm. Add the vegetables to the pan and stir-fry for 2–3 minutes. Remove with a slotted spoon and keep warm. Add the reserved marinade to the pan and cook, stirring until thickened. Return the beef and vegetables to the pan and heat through. Serve with rice or noodles.

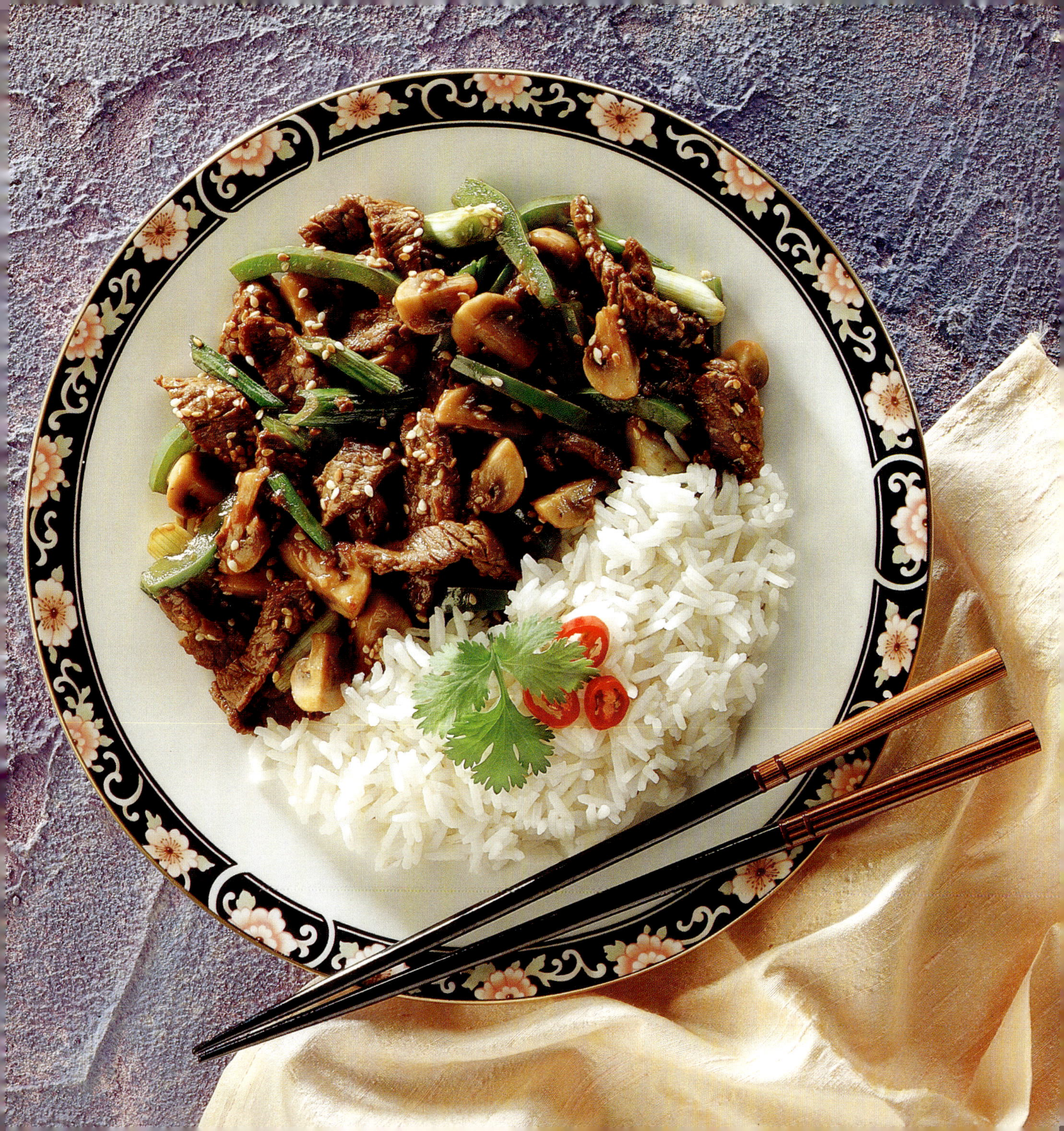

INDONESIAN PORK AND PRAWN RICE

Also known as Nasi Goreng, this is an attractive way of using up leftovers and appears in many variations throughout Indonesia. Rice is the main ingredient, and chillies and ginger are added for additional colour and flavour.

Serves 4–6

3 eggs
60ml/4 tbsp vegetable oil
6 shallots, or 1 large onion, chopped
2 garlic cloves, crushed
15ml/1 tbsp chopped fresh root ginger
3 small red chillies, seeded and chopped
15ml/1 tbsp fish sauce
2.5ml/½ tsp ground turmeric
30ml/2 tbsp creamed coconut
juice of 2 limes
10ml/2 tsp sugar
350g/12oz lean pork, sliced
350g/12oz fresh or cooked prawn tails
175g/6oz/¾ cup beansprouts
175g/6oz/2 cups Chinese leaves, shredded
115g/4oz/1 cup frozen peas, thawed
250g/9oz/1½ cups long grain rice, cooked
salt
chopped fresh coriander, to garnish

In a bowl, beat the eggs with a pinch of salt. Heat a non-stick frying pan over a moderate heat. Pour in the eggs and swirl around the pan to give a thin, even layer. Cook until set, roll up tightly, slice thinly, cover and set aside.

Heat 15ml/1 tbsp of the oil in a wok and fry the shallots or onion until evenly brown. Remove from pan, set aside and keep warm.

Heat the remaining 45ml/3 tbsp of oil in the wok, add the garlic, ginger and chillies and soften without colouring. Stir in the fish sauce, turmeric, coconut, lime juice, sugar and salt to taste. Combine briefly over a moderate heat. Add the pork and prawns and fry for 3–4 minutes.

Toss the beansprouts, Chinese leaves and peas in the spices and cook briefly. Add the rice and stir-fry for 6–8 minutes, stirring to prevent it from burning. Turn out on to a large serving plate, decorate with shredded omelette, the fried shallots or onion and chopped fresh coriander.

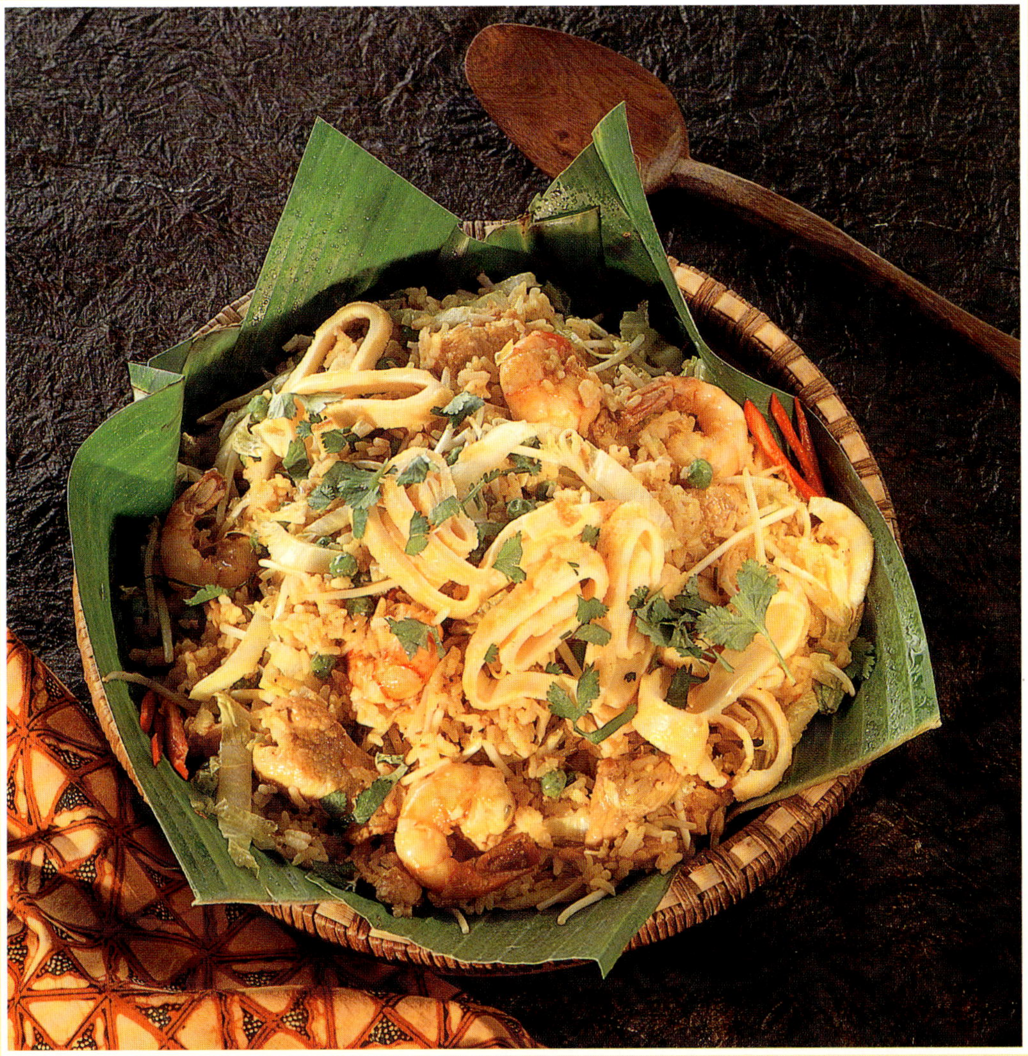

POULTRY AND MEAT

Beef Strips with Orange and Ginger

Tender strips of beef, tangy ginger and crisp carrot make a simple but delicious stir-fry.

Serves 4

450g/1lb lean beef rump, fillet or sirloin, cut into thin strips
finely grated rind and juice of 1 orange
15ml/1 tbsp light soy sauce
5ml/1 tsp cornflour
15ml/1 tbsp finely chopped root ginger
10ml/2 tsp sesame oil
1 large carrot, cut into thin strips
2 spring onions, thinly sliced

Place the beef strips in a bowl and sprinkle over the orange rind and juice. Leave to marinate for at least 30 minutes.

Drain the liquid from the meat and set aside, then mix the meat with the soy sauce, cornflour and ginger until well combined.

Heat the oil in a wok or large frying pan and add the beef. Stir-fry for 1 minute until lightly coloured, then add the carrot and continue to stir-fry for a further 2–3 minutes.

Stir in the spring onions and reserved liquid, then cook, stirring, until boiling and thickened. Serve hot with rice noodles or plain boiled rice.

Cook's tip
Large wok lids are cumbersome and can be difficult to store in a small kitchen. Instead of using a lid, place a circle of greaseproof paper over the food surface to retain the cooking juices.

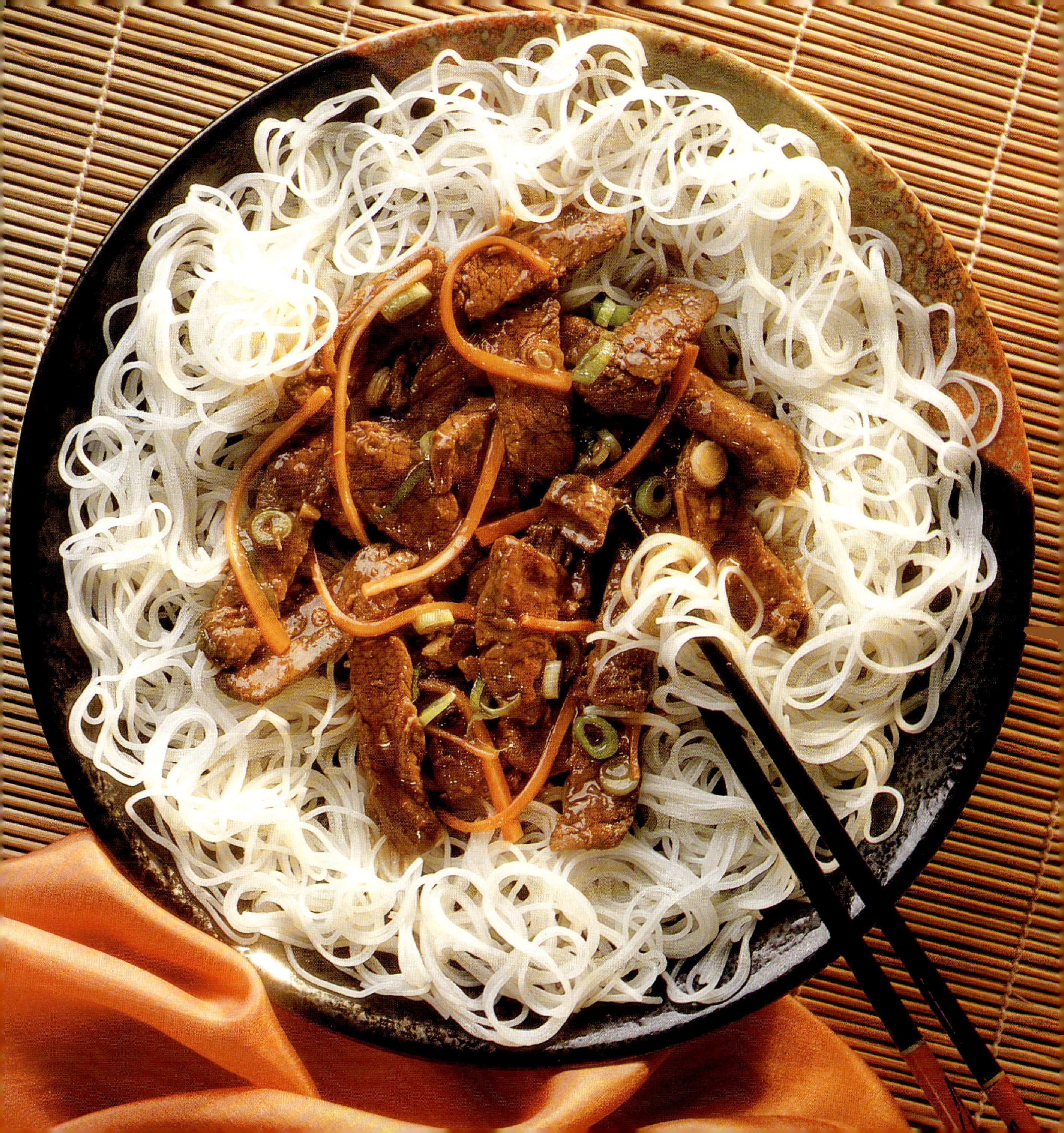

Ginger and Five-spice Lamb

Long, slow cooking in a rich mixture of spices is the secret of success with this aromatic lamb dish which is perfect for an informal supper party.

Serves 4

30–45ml/2–3 tbsp oil
1.5kg/3–3½lb leg of lamb, boned and cubed
1 onion, chopped
15ml/1 tbsp grated fresh root ginger
1 garlic clove, crushed
5ml/1 tsp five-spice powder
30ml/2 tbsp hoi-sin sauce
15ml/1 tbsp light soy sauce
300ml/½ pint/1¼ cups passata
250ml/8fl oz/1 cup lamb stock
1 red pepper, seeded and cubed
1 yellow pepper, seeded and cubed
30ml/2 tbsp chopped fresh coriander
15ml/1 tbsp sesame seeds, toasted
salt and ground black pepper

Preheat the oven to 160°C/325°F/Gas 3. Heat 30ml/2 tbsp of the oil in a flameproof casserole and brown the lamb in batches over a high heat. Remove with a slotted spoon and set aside.

Add the onion, ginger and garlic to the casserole with a little more of the oil, if necessary, and cook for about 5 minutes, until softened.

Return the lamb to the casserole. Stir in the five-spice powder, hoi-sin and soy sauces, passata, stock and seasoning. Bring to the boil, then cover and cook in the oven for 1¼ hours.

Remove the casserole from the oven, stir in the peppers, then cover and return to the oven for a further 15 minutes, or until the lamb is very tender.

Sprinkle with the coriander and sesame seeds. Serve hot.

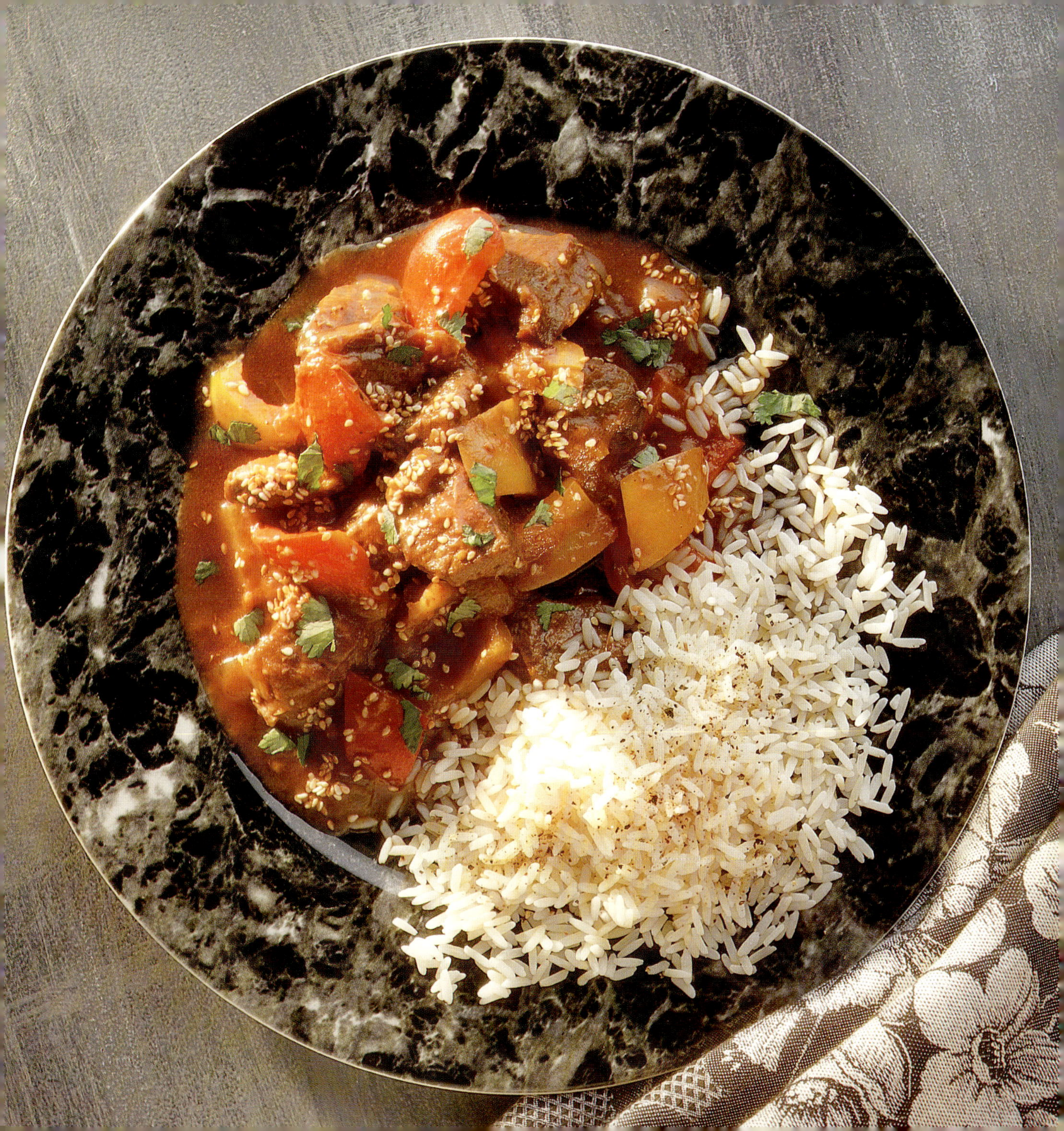

Vegetarian Dishes

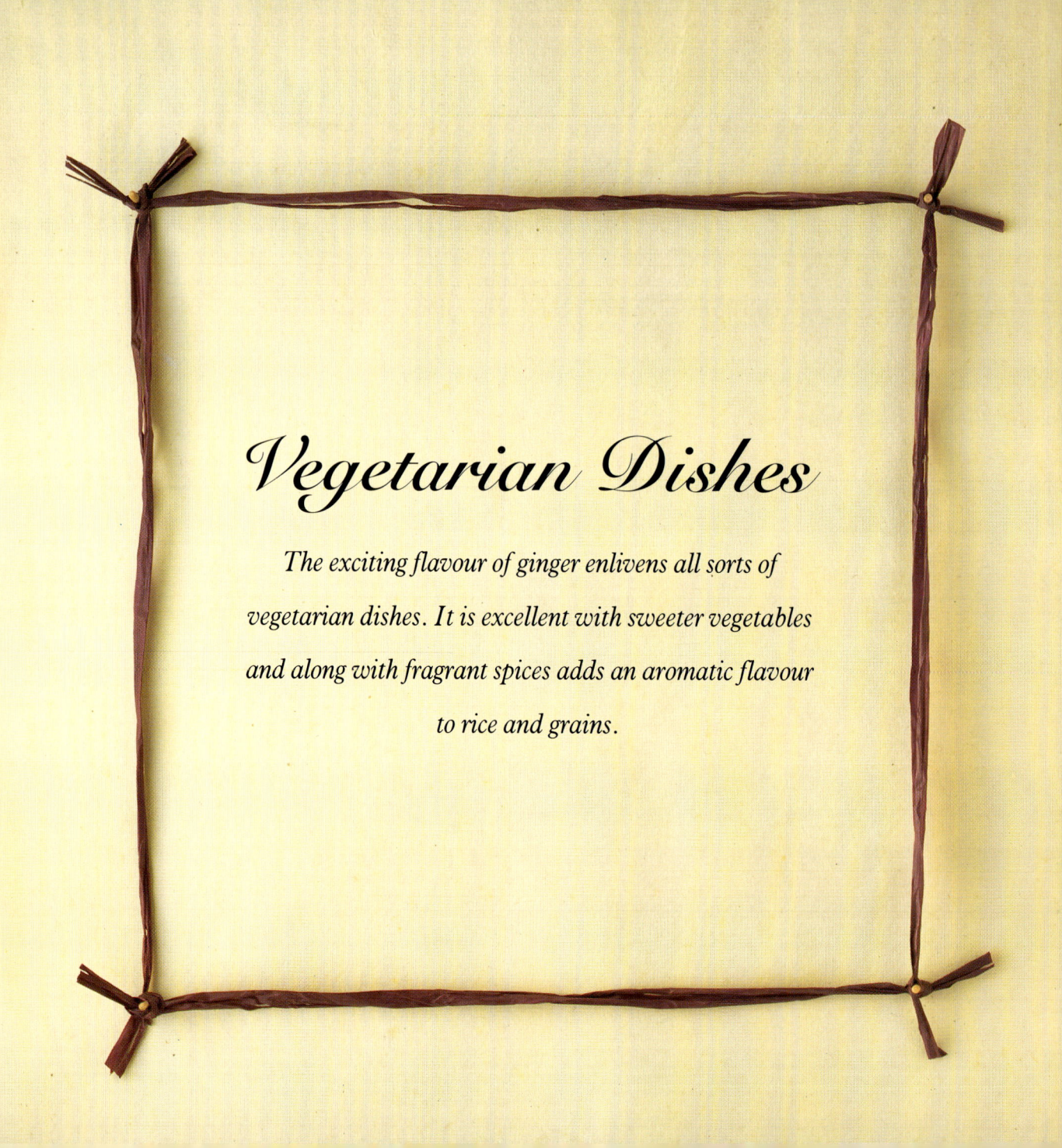

The exciting flavour of ginger enlivens all sorts of vegetarian dishes. It is excellent with sweeter vegetables and along with fragrant spices adds an aromatic flavour to rice and grains.

Vegetable Curry with Ginger

A tasty mid-week curry to serve with rice such as brown basmati, small poppadums and cucumber raita.

Serves 4

2 garlic cloves, chopped
15ml/1 tbsp chopped fresh root ginger
1 fresh green chilli, seeded and chopped
15ml/1 tbsp oil
1 onion, sliced
1 large potato, chopped
30ml/2 tbsp ghee or softened butter
15ml/1 tbsp curry powder, mild or hot
1 medium-size cauliflower, cut into small florets
600ml/1 pint/2½ cups stock
25g/1oz/2 tbsp creamed coconut
salt and ground black pepper
285g/10oz can broad beans, with liquid
juice of half a lemon (optional)
chopped fresh coriander or parsley, to serve

Put the garlic, ginger, chilli and oil in a blender or food processor and process until a smooth paste is formed.

In a large saucepan, fry the onion and potato in the ghee or butter for 5 minutes then stir in the spice paste and curry powder. Cook for 1 minute.

Add the cauliflower florets and stir well into the spicy mixture, then pour in the stock. Bring to the boil and mix in the coconut, stirring until it melts.

Season well then cover and simmer for 10 minutes. Add the beans and their liquid and cook uncovered for a further 10 minutes.

Check the seasoning and add a good squeeze of lemon juice if liked. Serve hot garnished with fresh coriander or parsley.

Herb Crepes with Tomato and Ginger Sauce

These mouth-watering light herb crêpes with ginger-flavoured sauce make a delicious starter, or serve with a crisp salad for a light lunch. Use a mixture of herbs such as parsley, thyme and chervil.

Serves 4

25g/1oz mixed chopped fresh herbs
a little sunflower oil
120ml/4fl oz/½ cup milk
3 eggs
25g/1oz/¼ cup plain flour
pinch of salt

For the sauce
30ml/2 tbsp olive oil
1 small onion, chopped
2 garlic cloves, crushed
15ml/1 tbsp grated fresh root ginger
400g/14oz can chopped tomatoes

For the filling
450g/1lb fresh spinach
175g/6oz/¾ cup ricotta cheese
30ml/2 tbsp pine nuts, toasted
5 sun-dried tomatoes, chopped
30ml/2 tbsp shredded fresh basil
salt, nutmeg and ground black pepper
4 egg whites

To make the crêpes, place the herbs and 15ml/1 tbsp oil in a blender or food processor and blend until smooth. Add the milk, eggs, flour and salt and blend again until smooth. Leave to rest for 30 minutes. Heat a small non-stick crêpe or frying pan and add a very small amount of oil. Pour out any excess oil and pour in a ladleful of the batter. Swirl to cover the base. Cook for 1–2 minutes, turn and cook the other side. Repeat to make 8 crêpes.

To make the sauce, heat the oil in a small pan. Add the onion, garlic and ginger and cook gently for 5 minutes until softened. Add the tomatoes and cook for a further 10–15 minutes until thickened. Purée in a blender or food processor, sieve and set aside. To make the filling, wash the spinach, removing any large stalks, and place in a large pan with only the water that clings to the leaves. Cover and cook until the spinach has just wilted. Remove from the heat and refresh in cold water. Place in a sieve, squeeze out the excess water and chop finely. Mix the spinach with the ricotta, pine nuts, sun-dried tomatoes and basil. Season with salt, nutmeg and pepper.

Preheat the oven to 190°C/375°F/Gas 5. Whisk the 4 egg whites until stiff but not dry. Fold one-third into the spinach and ricotta to lighten the mixture, then gently fold in the rest. Place a large spoonful of filling on each crêpe and fold into quarters. Place on an oiled baking sheet. Repeat until all the filling and crêpes are used up. Bake in the oven for 10–15 minutes or until set. Gently reheat the tomato sauce ready to serve with the crêpes.

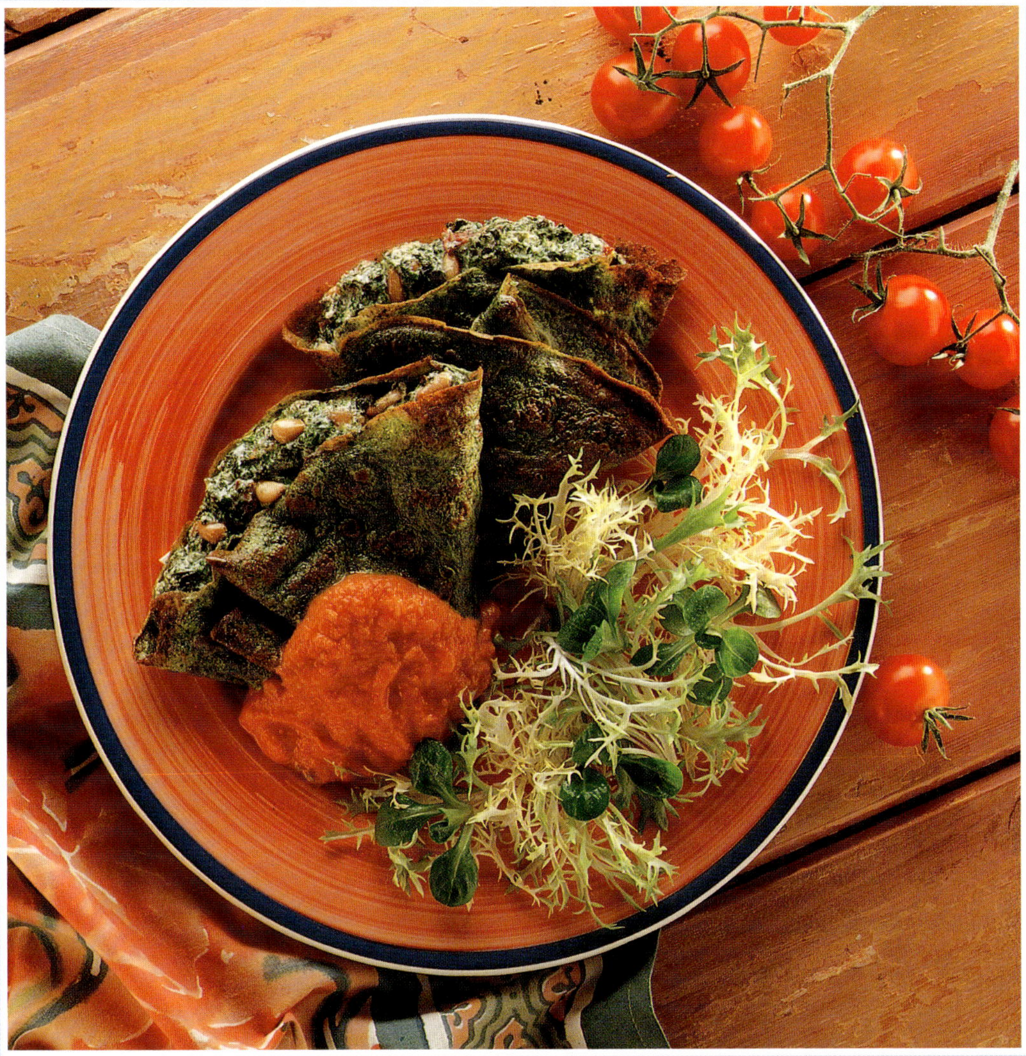

Mushroom and Okra Curry with Gingery Mango Relish

This simple but delicious curry with its fresh gingery mango relish is best served with plain basmati rice.

Serves 4

4 garlic cloves, chopped
15ml/1 tbsp chopped root ginger
1–2 red chillies, seeded and chopped
175ml/6fl oz/¾ cup cold water
15ml/1 tbsp sunflower oil
5ml/1 tsp coriander seeds
5ml/1 tsp cumin seeds
5ml/1 tsp ground cumin
2.5ml/½ tsp ground cardamom
pinch of ground turmeric
400g/14oz can chopped tomatoes
450g/1lb mushrooms, quartered if large
225g/8oz okra, trimmed and cut into 1cm/½in slices
30ml/2 tbsp chopped fresh coriander

For the mango relish
1 large ripe mango
1 small garlic clove, crushed
1 onion, finely chopped
10ml/2 tsp grated fresh root ginger
1 fresh red chilli, seeded and chopped
pinch of salt and sugar

For the mango relish, peel the mango and cut the flesh from the stone. In a bowl mash the mango flesh with a fork or use a blender or food processor, and mix in the rest of the relish ingredients. Set aside.

Place the garlic, ginger, chillies and 45ml/3 tbsp of the water into a blender or food processor and blend until smooth.

Heat the sunflower oil in a large pan. Add the whole coriander and cumin seeds and allow them to sizzle for a few seconds. Add the ground cumin, ground cardamom and turmeric and cook for 1 minute more.

Add the paste from the blender, the tomatoes, remaining water, mushrooms and okra. Stir to mix well and bring to the boil. Reduce the heat, cover, and simmer for 5 minutes.

Remove the cover, turn up the heat slightly and cook for a further 5–10 minutes until the okra is tender. Stir in the fresh coriander and serve with plain basmati rice and the mango relish.

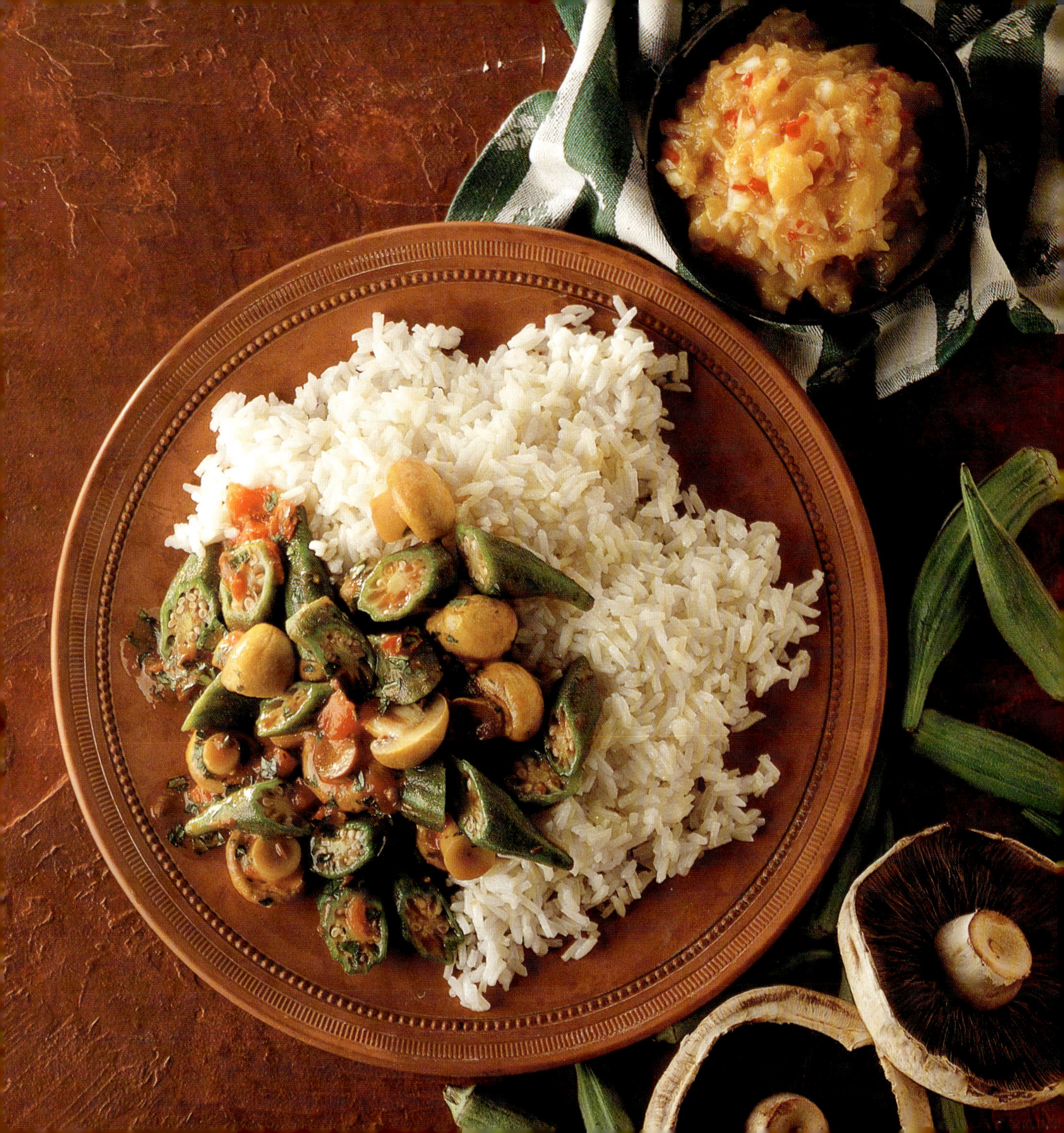

VEGETARIAN DISHES

THAI FRAGRANT RICE WITH GINGER

A lovely, soft, fluffy rice dish, perfumed with fresh ginger and lemon grass.

Serves 4

1 piece of lemon grass
2 limes
225g/8oz/1 cup brown basmati rice
15ml/1 tbsp olive oil
1 onion, chopped
15ml/1 tbsp chopped fresh root ginger
7.5ml/1½ tsp coriander seeds
7.5ml/1½ tsp cumin seeds
700ml/1¼ pints/3 cups vegetable stock
60ml/4 tbsp chopped fresh coriander
lime wedges, to serve

Finely chop the lemon grass. Remove the rind from the limes using a zester or fine grater. Rinse the rice in plenty of cold water until the water runs clear. Drain through a sieve. Heat the oil in a large pan and gently cook the onion, ginger, spices, lemon grass and lime rind for 2–3 minutes. Add the rice and cook for another minute, then add the stock and bring to the boil. Reduce the heat and cover the pan. Cook gently for 30 minutes then check the rice. If it is still crunchy, cover the pan again and leave for a further 3–5 minutes. Remove from the heat.

Stir in the fresh coriander, fluff up the grains, cover and leave for about 10 minutes. Serve hot, with lime wedges.

COOK'S TIP

Other varieties of rice, such as white basmati or long grain, can also be used for this dish but you will need to adjust the cooking times accordingly.

SPICY GINGER DHAL

If you thought yellow split peas were only for soups, then try this Indian-inspired dish. Serve with rice, chapatis or naan bread and whatever main dish you like.

Serves 4–6

225g/8oz yellow split peas
2 onions, chopped
1 large bay leaf
600ml/1 pint/2½ cups stock or water
10ml/2 tsp black mustard seeds
30ml/2 tbsp butter, melted
1 garlic clove, crushed
15ml/1 tbsp grated fresh root ginger
1 small green pepper, sliced
5ml/1 tsp ground turmeric
5ml/1 tsp garam masala or mild curry powder
3 tomatoes, skinned and chopped
salt and ground black pepper
fresh coriander or parsley, to serve

Put the split peas, 1 onion and the bay leaf in the stock or water, in a covered pan. Simmer for 25 minutes, seasoning lightly towards the end.

In a separate pan, fry the mustard seeds in the butter for about 30 seconds until they start to pop, then add all the remaining onion, along with the garlic, ginger and green pepper.

Sauté for about 5 minutes until softened then stir in the turmeric, garam masala or mild curry powder and fry for a few seconds more.

Add the split peas, tomatoes, and a little extra water if needed. Cover and simmer for a further 10 minutes, then check the seasoning and serve hot garnished with fresh coriander or parsley.

VEGETARIAN DISHES

Gingery Vegetable Couscous

This tasty combination of sweet vegetables and spices makes a hearty main dish.

Serves 4

1 generous pinch of saffron threads
15ml/1 tbsp olive oil
1 red onion, sliced
2 garlic cloves, crushed
1–2 fresh red chillies, seeded and finely chopped
15ml/1 tbsp chopped fresh root ginger
2.5ml/½ tsp ground cinnamon
400g/14oz can chopped tomatoes
300ml/½ pint/1¼ cups vegetable stock
4 carrots, sliced
2 turnips, cubed
450g/1lb sweet potatoes, cubed
75g/3oz/⅓ cup raisins
2 courgettes, sliced
400g/14oz can chick-peas, drained and rinsed
45ml/3 tbsp chopped fresh parsley
45ml/3 tbsp chopped fresh coriander
450g/1lb quick-cook couscous

Put the saffron in a small bowl and leave to infuse in 45ml/3 tbsp boiling water for about 30 minutes.

Heat the oil in a large saucepan. Add the onion, garlic and chillies and cook gently for 5 minutes until softened.

Add the chopped ginger and cinnamon and continue to cook for a further 1–2 minutes.

Add the tomatoes, stock, infused saffron and liquid, carrots, turnips, sweet potatoes and raisins, cover and simmer for 25 minutes.

Add the courgettes, chick-peas, parsley and coriander and cook for another 10 minutes until all the vegetables are cooked.

Meanwhile prepare the couscous following the packet instructions and serve with the vegetables.

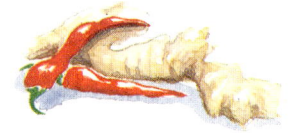

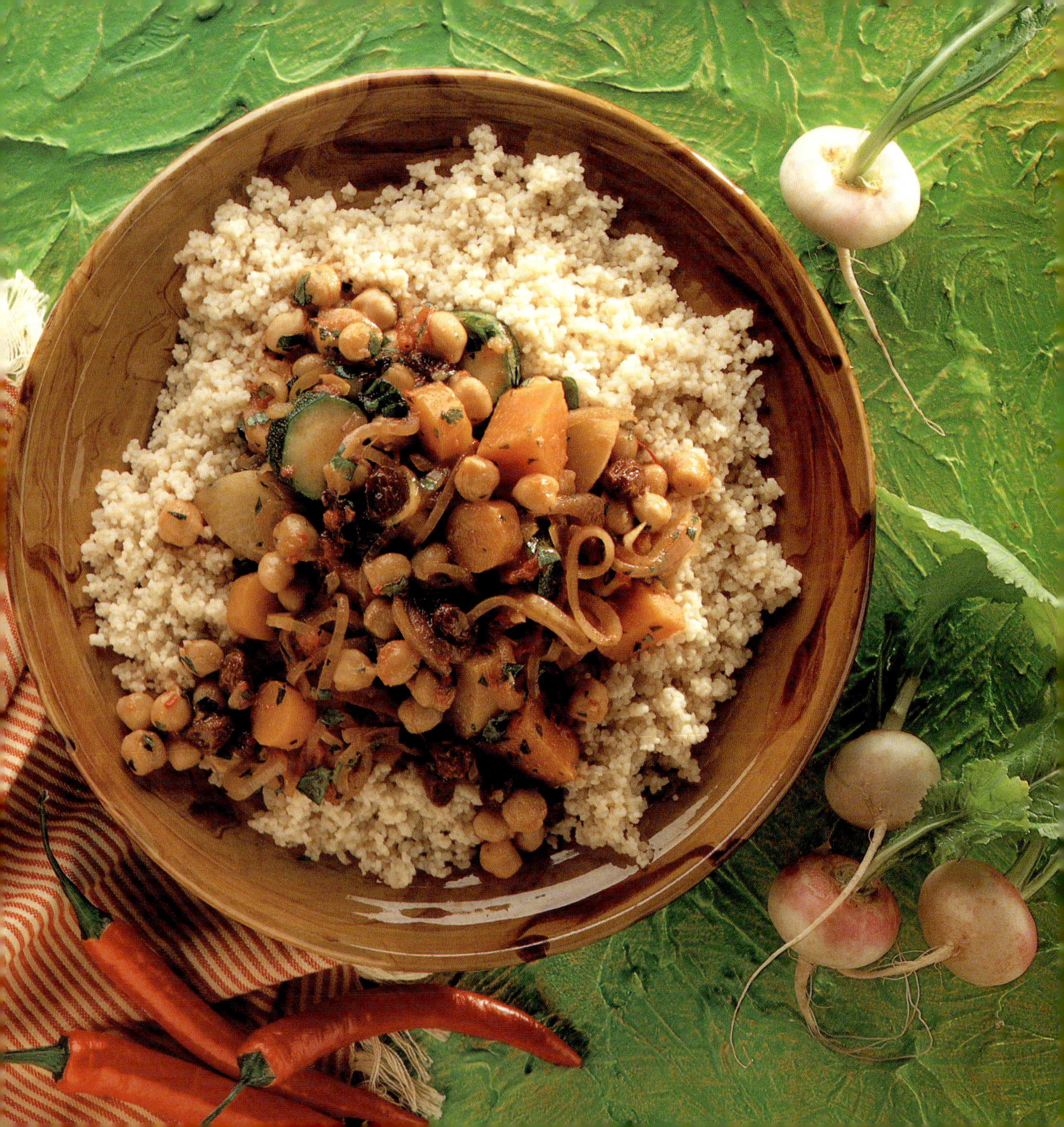

Lemon and Ginger Spicy Beans

An extremely quick delicious meal, made with canned beans for speed.

Serves 4

30ml/2 tbsp chopped fresh root ginger
3 garlic cloves, roughly chopped
250ml/8fl oz/1 cup cold water
15ml/1 tbsp sunflower oil
1 large onion, thinly sliced
1 fresh red chilli, seeded and finely chopped
1.5ml/¼ tsp cayenne pepper
10ml/2 tsp ground cumin
5ml/1 tsp ground coriander
2.5ml/½ tsp ground turmeric
30ml/2 tbsp lemon juice
15g/½oz/½ cup chopped fresh coriander
400g/14oz can black-eyed beans, drained and rinsed
400g/14oz can aduki beans, drained and rinsed
400g/14oz can haricot beans, drained and rinsed
salt and ground black pepper

Place the ginger, garlic and 60ml/4 tbsp of the cold water in a blender or food processor and blend until smooth. Set aside.

Heat the oil in a pan. Add the onion and red chilli and cook gently for about 5 minutes until softened.

Add the cayenne pepper, cumin, ground coriander and turmeric and stir-fry for 1 minute.

Stir in the ginger and garlic paste from the blender and cook for another minute, stirring to prevent sticking.

Add the remaining water, lemon juice and fresh coriander, stir well and bring to the boil. Cover the pan tightly and cook for 5 minutes.

Add all the beans and cook for a further 5–10 minutes. Season with salt and pepper to taste and serve.

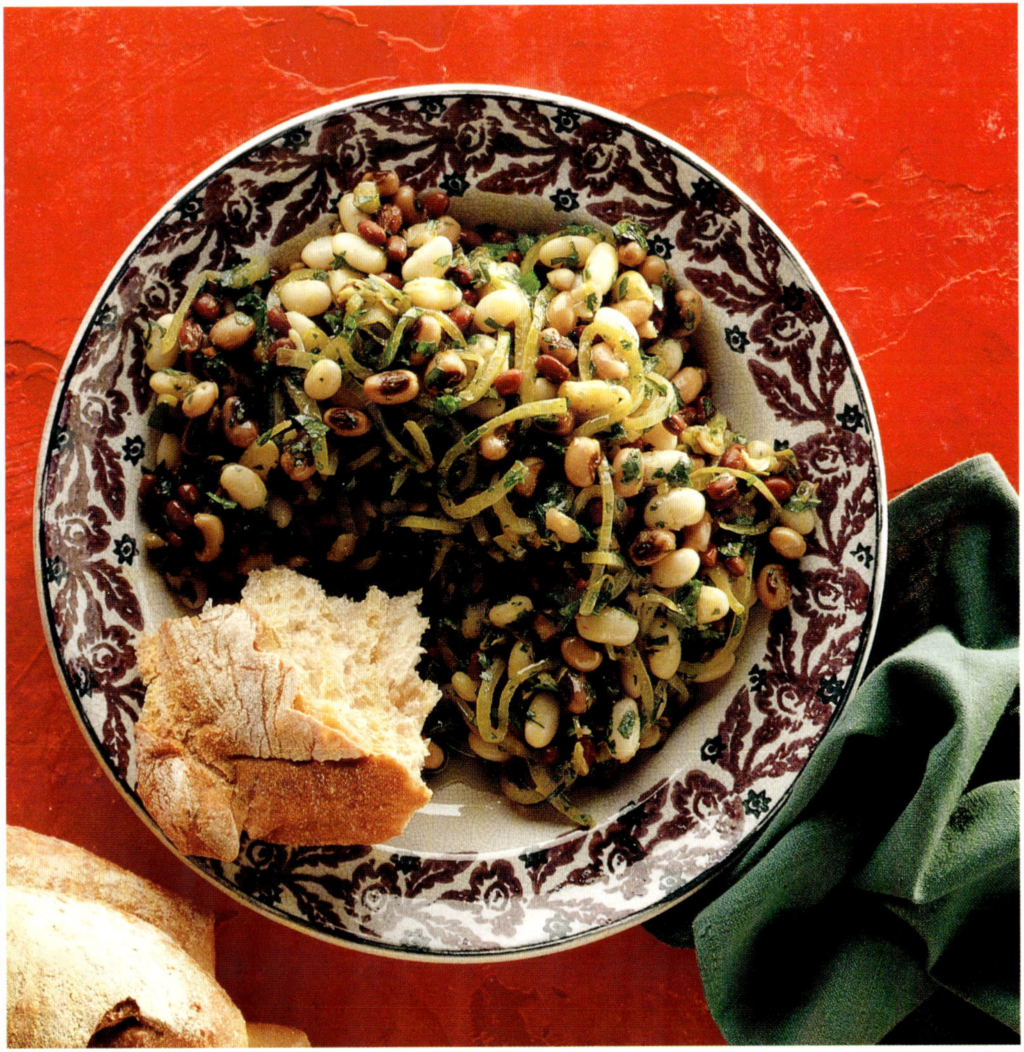

Desserts and Cakes

Syrupy stem ginger and freshly grated root ginger give a refreshing, if unexpected, bite to fruit desserts and ice cream. Ground ginger adds a warm mellow glow to home-baked cakes.

Golden Ginger Compote

Warm, spicy and full of sun-ripened ingredients – this is the perfect winter dessert.

Serves 4

200g/7oz/2 cups kumquats
200g/7oz/1¼ cups dried apricots
30ml/2 tbsp sultanas
400ml/14fl oz/1⅔ cups water
1 orange
15ml/1 tbsp grated fresh root ginger
4 green cardamom pods
4 cloves
30ml/2 tbsp clear honey
15ml/1 tbsp flaked almonds, toasted

Wash the kumquats, and, if they are large, cut them in half. Place them in a pan with the apricots, sultanas and water. Bring to the boil.

Pare the rind thinly from the orange and add to the pan. Add the ginger to the pan. Lightly crush the cardamom pods and add them to the pan, along with the cloves.

Reduce the heat, cover the pan and leave to simmer gently for about 30 minutes, or until the fruit is tender, stirring occasionally.

Squeeze the juice from the orange and add to the pan with honey to taste, sprinkle with flaked almonds and serve warm.

COOK'S TIP

Use ready-to-eat dried apricots. Reduce the liquid to 300ml/½ pint/1¼ cups, add apricots for the last 5 minutes of cooking.

Mango and Ginger Clouds

The sweet, perfumed flavour of ripe mango combines beautifully with ginger, and this low-fat dessert makes the very most of them both.

Serves 6

3 ripe mangoes
3 pieces stem ginger in syrup
45ml/3 tbsp stem ginger syrup
75g/3oz/½ cup silken tofu
3 egg whites
6 pistachios, chopped

Cut the mangoes in half and remove the stones. Peel and roughly chop the flesh. Put the mango flesh in a blender or food processor with the ginger, syrup and tofu. Blend until smooth. Spoon into a bowl. Put the egg whites in a bowl and whisk them until they form soft peaks. Fold the egg whites lightly into the mango mixture.

Spoon the mixture into wide dishes or glasses and chill well before serving, sprinkled with the chopped pistachios.

Variation
If you prefer, you can serve this dessert lightly frozen. Add the nuts just before serving.

Cook's Tip
Don't serve raw egg whites to pregnant women, babies, young children, the elderly, or anyone who is ill.

Watermelon, Ginger and Grapefruit Salad

The combination of fruit and ginger is very light and refreshing for a summer meal.

Serves 4

500g/1¼lb/2 cups diced watermelon flesh
2 ruby or pink grapefruit
2 pieces stem ginger in syrup
30ml/2 tbsp stem ginger syrup

Cook's tip

Toss the fruits gently – grapefruit segments will break up easily and the appearance of the dish will be spoiled.

Remove any seeds from the watermelon and cut the flesh into bite-size chunks. Using a small sharp knife, cut away all the peel and white pith from the grapefruits and carefully lift out the segments. Work over a bowl to catch any juice. Finely chop the stem ginger and place in a serving bowl with the melon cubes and grapefruit segments, adding the reserved juice. Spoon the ginger syrup over the fruits and toss lightly together before serving.

Gingerbread Upside-down Pudding

This old-fashioned, rich, gingery pudding is quite quick to make and looks very impressive.

Serves 4–6

sunflower oil, for brushing
15ml/1 tbsp soft brown sugar
4 medium peaches, halved and stoned, or canned peach halves
8 walnut halves

For the base
130g/4½oz/1 cup wholemeal flour
2.5ml/½ tsp bicarbonate of soda
7.5ml/1½ tsp ground ginger
5ml/1 tsp ground cinnamon
115g/4oz/½ cup molasses sugar
1 egg
125ml/4fl oz/½ cup skimmed milk
50ml/2fl oz/¼ cup sunflower oil

Preheat the oven to 180°C/350°F/Gas 4. For the topping, brush the base and sides of a 23cm/9in round springform tin with oil. Sprinkle the sugar over the base of the tin.

Arrange the peaches cut-side down in the tin with a walnut half in each.

For the base, sift together the flour, bicarbonate of soda, ginger and cinnamon, then stir in the sugar. Beat together the egg, milk and oil, then mix into the dry ingredients until smooth. Pour the mixture evenly over the peaches and bake for 35–40 minutes, until firm to the touch. Turn out on to a serving plate. Serve hot with yogurt or custard.

Ginger Ice Cream

Stem ginger adds a delicious spiciness to this creamy, refreshing ice cream.

Serves 4–6

475ml/16fl oz/2 cups milk
10cm/4in vanilla pod
4 egg yolks
75g/3oz/6 tbsp granulated sugar
4 pieces stem ginger, chopped
30ml/2 tbsp stem ginger syrup

Make the custard. Heat the milk with the vanilla pod in a small saucepan without letting it boil. Remove from the heat. Beat the egg yolks and gradually add the sugar. Beat for about 5 minutes. Add the milk gradually through a strainer, stirring constantly. Discard the vanilla pod. Pour the mixture into the top of a double boiler and add the chopped ginger. Stir over a moderate heat until the custard thickens enough to coat the back of a spoon. Add the ginger syrup. Remove from the heat and cool. Freeze in an ice-cream machine, or freeze, process and freeze again.

Banana Ginger Parkin

Parkin is a moist, sticky, ginger cake that keeps well and improves with keeping. Store it in a covered container for up to two months.

Makes 1 cake
200g/7oz/1¾ cups plain flour
10ml/2 tsp bicarbonate of soda
10ml/2 tsp ground ginger
150g/5oz/1¾ cups medium oatmeal
60ml/4 tbsp dark muscovado sugar
75g/3oz/6 tbsp sunflower margarine
150g/5oz/⅔ cup golden syrup
1 egg, beaten
3 ripe bananas, mashed
75g/3oz/¾ cup icing sugar
stem ginger, to decorate (optional)

Preheat the oven to 160°C/325°F/Gas 3. Grease an 18 × 28cm/7 × 11in cake tin and line base with greaseproof paper.

Sift together the flour, bicarbonate of soda and ginger, then stir in the oatmeal. Melt the sugar, margarine and syrup in a saucepan over a low heat, then leave to cool for a few minutes before stirring into the flour mixture. Beat in the egg and mashed bananas.

Spoon into the tin and bake for about 1 hour, or until firm to the touch. Allow to cool in the tin, then turn out and cut into squares.

Sift the icing sugar into a bowl and stir in just enough water to make a smooth, runny icing. Drizzle the icing over each square and top with pieces of stem ginger, if you like.

Cook's tip
This is a nutritious, energy-giving cake that is a really good choice for packed lunches as it doesn't break up too easily.

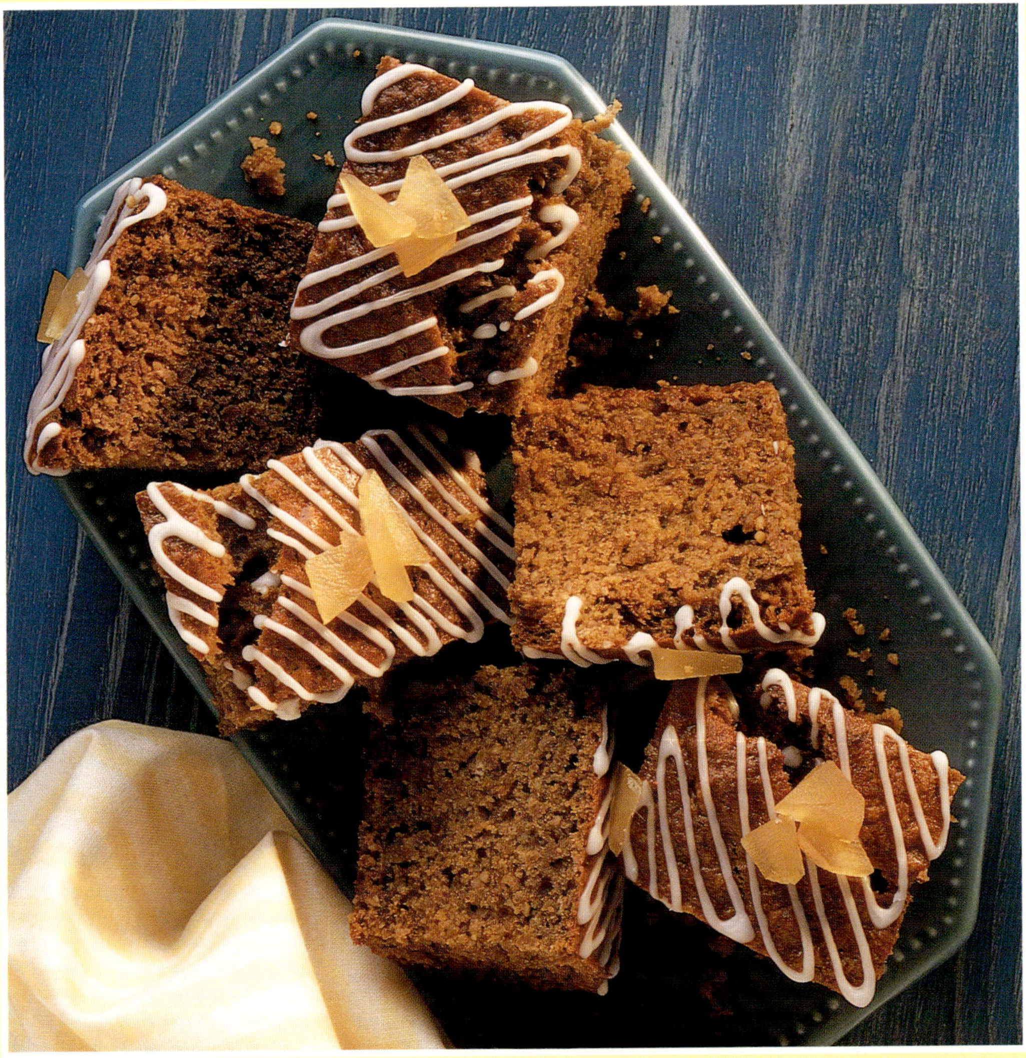

Pineapple and Ginger Cake

This tasty cake is packed with flavours; apricot and pineapple are combined with tangy orange and lemon and spiked with the refreshing, peppery taste of ginger.

Serves 10–12

175g/6oz/¾ cup unsalted butter
150g/5oz/¾ cup caster sugar
3 eggs, beaten
few drops vanilla essence
225g/8oz/2 cups plain flour, sifted
1.5ml/¼ tsp salt
7.5ml/1½ tsp baking powder
225g/8oz/1⅓ cups ready-to-eat dried apricots, chopped
115g/4oz/½ cup each chopped crystallized ginger and crystallized pineapple
grated rind and juice of ½ orange
grated rind and juice of ½ lemon
a little milk

Cook's tip
This is not a long-keeping cake, but it does freeze, well-wrapped in greaseproof paper and then overwrapped in foil.

Preheat the oven to 180°C/350°F/Gas 4. Double line a 20cm/8in round or 18cm/7in square cake tin. Cream the butter and sugar together until the mixture is light and fluffy.

Gradually beat the eggs into the creamed mixture with the vanilla essence, beating well after each addition. Sift together the flour, salt and baking powder into a bowl, and add a little to the mixture with the last of the egg, then fold in the rest.

Fold in the fruit, ginger and fruit rinds gently, then add sufficient fruit juice and milk to give a fairly soft dropping consistency.

Spoon into the prepared tin and smooth the top with a wet spoon. Bake for 20 minutes, then reduce the oven temperature to 160°C/325°F/Gas 3 for a further 1½–2 hours, or until firm to the touch and a skewer comes out of the centre clean.

Leave the cake to cool in the tin, then turn out and wrap in fresh paper before storing in an airtight tin.

Index

Apricots: golden ginger compote, 55

Banana ginger parkin, 60
Beans: lemon and ginger spicy beans, 52
Beef: beef strips with orange and ginger, 38
  Chinese-style beef with ginger, 34

Chicken: chicken biryani, 32
  chicken with ginger couscous, 28
  gingery Chinese chicken wings, 18
  stir-fried ginger chicken, 30
  Thai chicken and prawn soup, 16
  Thai chicken and vegetable stir-fry, 27
Couscous: chicken with ginger couscous, 28
  gingery vegetable couscous, 50
Curry: mushroom and okra curry with gingery mango relish, 46
  vegetable curry with ginger, 43

Fish: fish with mango and ginger dressing, 21
  seafood kebabs with ginger and lime, 24

Gingerbread upside-down pudding, 58
Grapefruit: watermelon, ginger and grapefruit salad, 57

Herb crêpes with tomato and ginger sauce, 44

Ice cream: ginger ice cream, 59

Kumquats: golden ginger compote, 55

Lamb: ginger and five-spice lamb, 40
Leek, parsnip and ginger soup, 15
Lemon and ginger spicy beans, 52

Mango: fish with mango and ginger dressing, 21
  grilled snapper with mango salsa, 22
  mango and ginger clouds, 56
  mushroom and okra curry with gingery mango relish, 46
Mushroom and okra curry with gingery mango relish, 46

Okra: mushroom and okra curry with gingery mango relish, 46

Parsnips: leek, parsnip and ginger soup, 15
Peanuts: spicy peanut and ginger bites, 19

Pineapple and ginger cake, 62
Prawns: Indonesian pork and prawn rice, 36
  seafood kebabs with ginger and lime, 24
  Thai chicken and prawn soup, 16
Red snapper: grilled snapper with mango salsa, 22
Rhubarb and ginger jam, 13
Rice: Indonesian pork and prawn rice, 36
  spicy peanut and ginger bites, 19
  Thai fragrant rice with ginger, 48

Scallops: scallops with ginger relish, 23
Split peas: spicy ginger dhal, 49

Tofu: mango and ginger clouds, 56
Tomatoes: herb crêpes with tomato and ginger sauce, 44

Vegetables: gingery vegetable couscous, 50
  Thai chicken and vegetable stir-fry, 27
  vegetable curry with ginger, 43

Watermelon, ginger and grapefruit salad, 57